Tell a Story/ Sing a Song

AUTHORS

Elaine Mei Aoki
•
Virginia A. Arnold
•
James Flood
•
James V. Hoffman
•
Diane Lapp
•
Miriam Martinez
•
Annemarie Sullivan Palincsar
•
Michael Priestley
•
Carl B. Smith
•
William H. Teale
•
Josefina Villamil Tinajero
•
Arnold W. Webb
•
Karen D. Wood

Macmillan McGraw-Hill

New York   Farmington

AUTHORS, CONSULTANTS

MULTICULTURAL AND EDUCATIONAL CONSULTANTS

Yvonne Beamer, Joyce Buckner, Alma Flor Ada, Helen Gillotte,
Cheryl Hudson, Narcita Medina, Lorraine Monroe, James R. Murphy,
Sylvia Peña, Joseph B. Rubin, Ramon Santiago, Cliff Trafzer,
Hai Tran, Esther Lee Yao

LITERATURE CONSULTANTS

Ashley Bryan, Joan I. Glazer, Paul Janeczko, Margaret H. Lippert

INTERNATIONAL CONSULTANTS

Edward B. Adams, Barbara Johnson, Raymond L. Marshall

MUSIC AND AUDIO CONSULTANTS

John Farrell, Marilyn C. Davidson, Vincent Lawrence,
Sarah Pirtle, Susan R. Snyder,
Rick and Deborah Witkowski

Macmillan/McGraw-Hill

A Division of The **McGraw·Hill** Companies

Macmillan/McGraw-Hill
1221 Avenue of the Americas
New York, New York 10020

Printed in the United States of America

ISBN 0-02-181364-7 / K, U.5

2 3 4 5 6 7 8 9 BCM 02 01 00 99 98 97

Teacher's Planning Guide

*This guide is dedicated as a tribute to all teachers who,
like Florence Zamarelli, one of my significant teachers,
encouraged many children to dream their dreams and
always to question the "why's" of life.
She taught us to believe that in search of
these dreams and answers
we would become friends with many wonderful books
and also gain the knowledge and inner beat
needed to create at least a few of our own.*

— Diane Lapp

Contents

Sing and Dance Away!
A theme about singing and dancing
Theme Words: SINGER and DANCER
Theme Poem: "Singing-Time"
  by Rose Fyleman
Theme Song: "You'll Sing a Song and I'll Sing a Song"
  by Ella Jenkins

2

Contents

4

INTRODUCING TELL A STORY/SING A SONG

A New View of Kindergarten!

Welcome children to a print-rich, activity-based environment that nurtures emergent literacy!

19 BIG BOOKS!

48 TRADE BOOKS!

16 THEMES!

PROGRAM RESOURCES

Big Book of Songs
Theme Songs!

Big Book of Poems
Theme Poems!

The more we get together,
Together, together,
The more we get together,
The happier we'll be.

For your friends are my friends,
And my friends are your friends.
The more we get together,
The happier we'll be.

Traditional

THE MORE WE GET TOGETHER

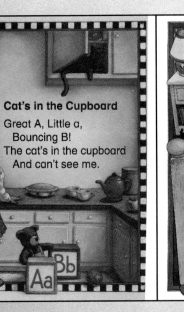

Cc

Cat's in the Cupboard

Great A, Little a,
Bouncing B!
The cat's in the cupboard
And can't see me.

Dd

Diddle Diddle Dumpling

Diddle diddle dumpling,
my son John
Went to bed with his
trousers on,
One shoe off,
and one shoe on;
Diddle diddle dumpling,
my son John.

Plus—

STAFF DEVELOPMENT

A to EZ Handbook:
Staff Development Guide

**Performance
Assessment Handbook**

**Early Literacy
Assessment**

Big Book of Alphabet Rhymes and Chimes
Verses for teaching the alphabet and concepts of print!
Plus the "Alphabet Song"!

Rhyme and Chime Strips
Each Rhyme and Chime
on illustrated strips to use in
pocket charts for
Hands On! Language
experiences!

Cat's in the Cupboard

Great A, Little a,

Bouncing B!

The cat's in the cupboard

And can't see me.

A a A a

B b B b

C c C c

**Teacher's Read Aloud
Anthology**
32 Read Aloud selections
from cultures around
the world!

16 LITERATURE THEME PACKS

including 3 Trade Books (1 with a companion Big Book) and a Teacher's Planning Guide!

"Slither," said the snake in the cool morning air.

"Twitter," said the sparrows. "Trot," said the mare.

Big Book of "Paddle," Said the Swan

"Paddle," Said the Swan

Written and Illust. Gloria Kar...

IN THE PARK
An Excursion in Four Languages
by ESTHER HAUTZIG
Pictures by EZRA JACK KEATS

Big Talk
By Miriam Schlein
Pictures by Joan Auclair

Also Available—

LISTENING LIBRARY AUDIOCASSETTES for Big Books!

SONGS AND STORIES AUDIOCASSETTES with Theme Songs, sound effects, and storytellings!

SING A SOUND AUDIOCASSETTES with songs to encourage language play and to develop phonemic awareness!

TEACHER'S PLANNING GUIDE

SPEAK OUT!
MACMILLAN/McGRAW-HILL

Teacher's Planning Guide for Speak Out!
Your resource for organizing activities—
• Sharing Time
• Reading and Writing
• Exploring Print
• Into the Learning Centers

ANCILLARIES

ABC Cards
Textured letter forms
for tactile learning!

Literature Activity Book with
- Activities for introducing
  each theme
- Tell-a-Tale Take-Home Books
- Responding to Literature pages
- Exploring Print activities
- Just for Fun pages, too!

Alphabet Posters
26 full-color posters!

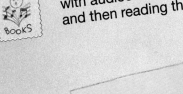

Sing & Read Books and Audiocassettes
16 little books, one for each theme song,
with audiocassettes of children singing
and then reading the selection!

Also Available —

HomeWords:
Newsletters and more
to send home each month!

Sights & Sounds:
Interactive software for children to use in their
exploration of the sounds of language
and the letters that represent them!

Program Themes	Trade Books	Read Alouds
1 GETTING TOGETHER	**BIG BOOK:** *Getting Together* by George Ancona *What Will Mommy Do When I'm at School?* by Dolores Johnson *I'm Busy, Too* by Norma Simon, illustrated by Dora Leder	**The Great Big Enormous Turnip** a Russian tale by Alexei Tolstoi **The Rabbit and the Elephant** a folk tale from Ghana retold by Ruthilde Kronberg and Patricia C. McKissack
2 SHARING WITH FRIENDS	**BIG BOOK:** *Frog in the Middle* by Susanna Gretz *Will I Have a Friend?* by Miriam Cohen, illustrated by Lillian Hoban *Friends* by Helme Heine	**The Lion and the Mouse** a fable by Aesop **The Three Friends** a folk tale from India retold by Isabel Wyatt
3 SPEAK OUT!	**BIG BOOK:** *"Paddle," Said the Swan* by Gloria Kamen *In the Park* by Esther Hautzig, illustrated by Ezra Jack Keats *Big Talk* by Miriam Schlein, illustrated by Joan Auclair	**The Long One** a Masai tale from East Africa by Verna Aardema **The Boy Who Cried Wolf** a fable by Aesop retold by Anne Terry White
4 LISTEN FOR SOUNDS!	**BIG BOOK:** *Rain Talk* by Mary Serfozo, illustrated by Keiko Narahashi *Country Crossing* by Jim Aylesworth, illustrated by Ted Rand *Apt. 3* by Ezra Jack Keats	**The Bremen Town Musicians** a German folk tale retold by Anne Rockwell **The Race Between Toad and Donkey** a Jamaican folk tale edited by Roger D. Abrahams

THEME WORDS	THEME SONGS	THEME POEMS	EXPLORING PRINT LESSONS
HELPER	**The More We Get Together** a traditional song	**Together** by Paul Engle	Games and activities related to children's names
FRIEND	**Be a Friend** a traditional song	**Making Friends** by Eloise Greenfield	Games and activities related to friends and their names, and days of the week
SPEAKER	**The Buenas Song** a Hispanic song by Aaron Schroeder and David Grover	**Good Morning** by Muriel Sipe	Rhyme Time: Games, songs, and activities for rhyming
LISTENER	**The Little Red Caboose** Bernice Johnson Reagon's version of the traditional song	**Ears Hear** by Lucia and James L. Hymes, Jr.	*Big Book of Alphabet Rhymes and Chimes:* **Cc** Cat's in the Cupboard **Pp** Pease Porridge Hot

PROGRAM THEMES	TRADE BOOKS	READ ALOUDS
5 SING AND DANCE AWAY!	**BIG BOOK:** *Oh, A-Hunting We Will Go* by John Langstaff, illustrated by Nancy Winslow Parker *Max* by Rachel Isadora *The Little Band* by James Sage, illustrated by Keiko Narahashi	**The Twelve Dancing Princesses** a German fairy tale by the Brothers Grimm **The Clever Turtle** a Hispanic folk tale retold by Margaret H. Lippert
6 PAINT IT UP!	**BIG BOOK:** *Who Said Red?* by Mary Serfozo, illustrated by Keiko Narahashi *The little Bear Book* by Anthony Browne *circles, triangles and squares* by Tana Hoban	**The Black Cat** an American folk tale retold by Margaret H. Lippert **Ma Lien and the Magic Brush** a tale from China by Hisako Kimishima retold by Alvin Tresselt
7 EAT IT UP!	**BIG BOOK:** *Bread, Bread, Bread* by Ann Morris, photographs by Ken Heyman *Gregory, the Terrible Eater* by Mitchell Sharmat, illustrated by Jose Aruego and Ariane Dewey *What's on My Plate?* by Ruth Belov Gross, illustrated by Isadore Seltzer	**The Woman Who Flummoxed the Fairies** a Scottish folk tale retold by Sorche Nic Leodhas **Señor Billy Goat** a Hispanic folk tale retold by Pura Belpré
8 BUILD IT UP!	**BIG BOOK:** *Changes, Changes* by Pat Hutchins *I Read Signs* by Tana Hoban *Round Trip* by Ann Jonas	**The Three Little Pigs** an English fairy tale retold by Flora Annie Steel **Why the Moon Is in the Sky** an Ashanti folk tale from West Africa retold by Margaret H. Lippert

THEME WORDS	THEME SONGS	THEME POEMS	EXPLORING PRINT LESSONS
SINGER DANCER	You'll Sing a Song and I'll Sing a Song by Ella Jenkins	Singing-Time by Rose Fyleman	*Big Book of Alphabet Rhymes and Chimes:* **Hh** Hippity Hop to Bed **Mm** Miss Mary Mack
ARTIST	I Know the Colors in the Rainbow by Ella Jenkins	Paints by Ilo Orleans	*Big Book of Alphabet Rhymes and Chimes:* **Ss** Sing a Song of Sixpence **Bb** Bounce High, Bounce Low
COOK	Short'ning Bread a traditional Southern song	Through the Teeth a folk rhyme	*Big Book of Alphabet Rhymes and Chimes:* **Gg** Gobble, Gobble **Aa** Eat an Apple
BUILDER	Johnny Builds with One Hammer a traditional song	Buildings by Myra Cohn Livingston	*Big Book of Alphabet Rhymes and Chimes:* **Rr** R Is for Ribbon **Ee** Engine, Engine, Number Nine

PROGRAM THEMES	TRADE BOOKS	READ ALOUDS
9 MEET PAT HUTCHINS	**BIG BOOK:** *Titch* by Pat Hutchins *Rosie's Walk* by Pat Hutchins *Good-Night, Owl!* by Pat Hutchins	**It Could Always Be Worse** a Yiddish folk tale retold by Margot Zemach **Rainbow Crow** a Lenape tale retold by Nancy Van Laan
10 SHARE A STORY!	**BIG BOOK:** *I Had a Cat* by Mona Rabun Reeves, illustrated by Julie Downing *Little Red Hen* by Janina Domanska *Nessa's Fish* by Nancy Luenn, illustrated by Neil Waldman	**The Storytelling Stone** a Seneca tale retold by Joseph Bruchac **The Three Bears** an English folk tale retold by Margaret H. Lippert
11 ACT IT OUT!	**BIG BOOK:** *Handtalk Zoo* by George Ancona and Mary Beth *Stone Soup* by Marcia Brown *I'm Going on a Dragon Hunt* by Maurice Jones, illustrated by Charlotte Firmin	**The Three Billy Goats Gruff** a Norwegian folk tale retold by Margaret H. Lippert **The Terrible Tragadabas** a tale from Spanish New Mexico by Joe Hayes
12 WONDER ABOUT IT!	**BIG BOOK:** *White Is the Moon* by Valerie Greeley *Half a Moon and One Whole Star* by Crescent Dragonwagon, illustrated by Jerry Pinkney *The Park Bench* by Fumiko Takeshita, illustrated by Mamoru Suzuki	**The Spider Weaver** a folk tale from Japan retold by Florence Sakada **The One You Don't See Coming** a folk tale from Liberia retold by Harold Courlander and George Herzog

THEME WORDS	THEME SONGS	THEME POEMS	EXPLORING PRINT LESSONS
WRITER	**Read a Book** by Marcy Marxer	**Surprise** by Beverly McLoughland	*Big Book of Alphabet Rhymes and Chimes:* **Tt** Toaster Time **Kk** A Kettle's for the Kitchen
STORYTELLER	**How About You?** by John Farrell	**Worlds I Know** by Myra Cohn Livingston	*Big Book of Alphabet Rhymes and Chimes:* **Ff** Five Little Fishies **Yy** The Yak
ACTOR	**Eency, Weency Spider** a traditional song	**On Our Way** by Eve Merriam	*Big Book of Alphabet Rhymes and Chimes:* **Qq** Quack, Quack, Quack **Zz** Zippety! Zippety! Zim, zim, zim!
THINKER	**Twinkle, Twinkle, Little Star** a traditional song	**I Arise** an Eskimo song	*Big Book of Alphabet Rhymes and Chimes:* **Ii** If All the World Was Apple Pie **Xx** What Words Begin with X?

PROGRAM THEMES	TRADE BOOKS	READ ALOUDS
13 FIND IT OUT!	**BIG BOOK:** *What Do You See?* by Janina Domanska *Farm Animals* photographs by Philip Dowell and Michael Dunning *Changes* by Marjorie N. Allen and Shelley Rotner, photographs by Shelley Rotner	**Why Bears Have Short Tails** a Navajo legend from Arizona retold by Sandra Begay **The Plumage of the Owl/ El Plumaje del Mucaro** a Puerto Rican folk tale retold by Ricardo E. Alegría
14 MEET EZRA JACK KEATS	**BIG BOOK:** *Hi, Cat!* by Ezra Jack Keats *Kitten for a Day* by Ezra Jack Keats *Pet Show!* by Ezra Jack Keats	**Belling the Cat** a fable by Aesop retold by Joseph Jacobs **The Cat's Purr** a West Indian tale by Ashley Bryan
15 THINKING ABOUT ME	**BIG BOOK:** *All I Am* by Eileen Roe, illustrated by Helen Cogancherry *The Train to Lulu's* by Elizabeth Fitzgerald Howard, illustrated by Robert Casilla *Con Mi Hermano/With My Brother* by Eileen Roe, illustrated by Robert Casilla	**The Knee-High Man** an American black folk tale retold by Julius Lester **Anansi's Rescue from the River** a folk tale from West Africa retold by Harold Courlander
16 SETTING OUT!	**BIG BOOK:** *As the Crow Flies: A First Book of Maps* by Gail Hartman, illustrated by Harvey Stevenson *Look Out, Patrick!* by Paul Geraghty *Builder of the Moon* by Tim Wynne-Jones, illustrated by Ian Wallace	**Timimoto** a folk tale from Japan retold by Margaret H. Lippert **Jack and the Beanstalk** an English fairy tale retold by Virginia Haviland

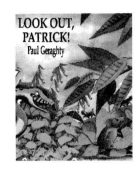

THEME WORDS	THEME SONGS	THEME POEMS	EXPLORING PRINT LESSONS
RESEARCHER	Who Fed the Chickens? by Ella Jenkins	Who? by Lilian Moore	*Big Book of Alphabet Rhymes and Chimes:* **Dd** Diddle Diddle Dumpling **Ww** Wee Willie Winkie
ILLUSTRATOR	Library Song by Michael Mark and Tom Chapin	Picture People by Myra Cohn Livingston	*Big Book of Alphabet Rhymes and Chimes:* **Ll** Lily's a Lady **Jj** Jack Be Nimble
CHILD	I Am a Person by Sarah Pirtle	By Myself by Eloise Greenfield	*Big Book of Alphabet Rhymes and Chimes:* **Nn** Nicholas Ned **Uu** Umbrellas
EXPLORER	The Bear Went Over the Mountain a traditional song	Come Out by Karla Kuskin	*Big Book of Alphabet Rhymes and Chimes:* **Oo** Polly, Put the Kettle On **Vv** Very Nice

Emergent Writing

MIRIAM MARTINEZ AND WILLIAM TEALE

The emergent literacy perspective is a powerful one because it lays the foundation for promoting children's literacy development through rich, exciting, and purposeful writing opportunities in the classroom.

1. **Drawing**

2. **Scribble**

Children's Writing Strategies

In their early explorations of the writing system, young children typically do not write in conventional ways. Careful observations of children's emergent writing have revealed a general, but rather complicated, developmental pathway. As children move along this pathway, they typically use some or all of the following strategies:

1. **Drawing**

2. **Scribbling**

3. **Randomly Chosen Letters:** The child uses letters, but there is not a relationship between the letters chosen and the sounds in the words that are written.

4. **Words Copied from Environmental Print**

5. **Developmental Spelling:** There is a relationship between the letters used and the sounds in the words that are written, but only one or two of the sounds heard in words are represented. This behavior later develops to the point at which children are able to use a letter to represent every (or almost every) sound in the words that are written.

6. **Transitional Spelling:** Features of conventional spelling, like silent letters or doubling of consonants, begin to appear.

7. **Conventional Spelling**

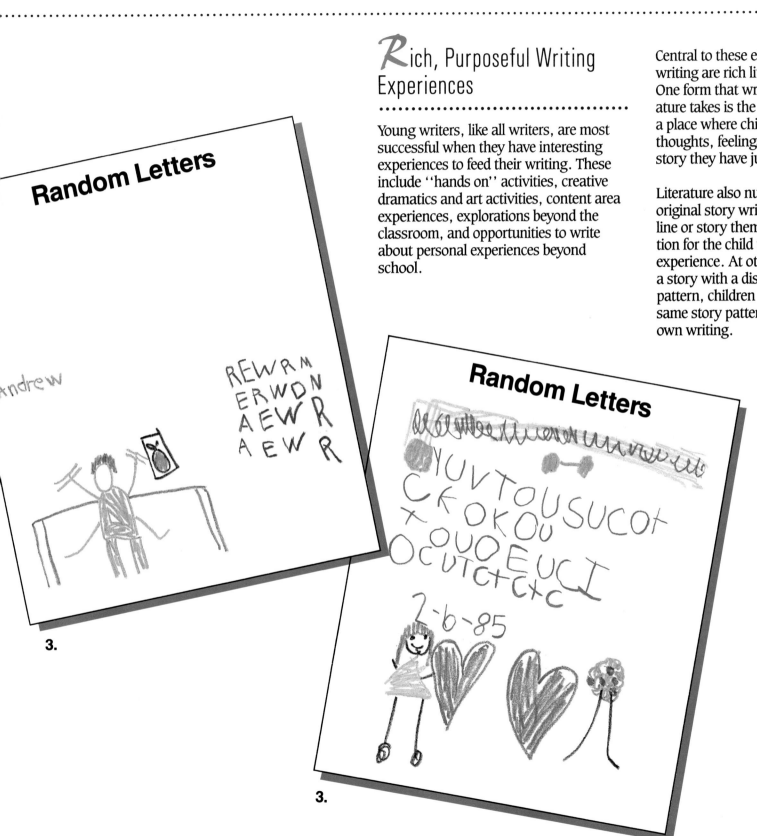

Random Letters

Andrew

REWRM
ERWDN
AEWR
AEWR

3.

*R*ich, Purposeful Writing Experiences

Young writers, like all writers, are most successful when they have interesting experiences to feed their writing. These include "hands on" activities, creative dramatics and art activities, content area experiences, explorations beyond the classroom, and opportunities to write about personal experiences beyond school.

Central to these efforts to ignite children's writing are rich literature experiences. One form that writing in response to literature takes is the journal. The journal is a place where children can record their thoughts, feelings, and reactions to a story they have just listened to or read.

Literature also nurtures children's own original story writing. Sometimes a story-line or story theme will serve as an invitation for the child to write about a similar experience. At other times, after reading a story with a distinctive predictable pattern, children may choose to use the same story pattern to organize their own writing.

Random Letters

YUVTOUSUCOt
CKOKOU
tOUOEUCI
OCUTCtCtC

2-6-85

3.

MERGENT WRITING

Children's Growth as Writers

Three dimensions signal growth in children's writing. First is evidence that the child is using increasingly more sophisticated writing strategies (drawing, scribbling, developmental spellings, and so on.). However, as we observe children's movement along this developmental pathway, it's important to remember that not every child uses all strategies, nor will a child necessarily, as he or she begins to use a more sophisticated strategy, leave less sophisticated ones behind. If anything, many children tend to expand their repertoire of strategies, using different ones for different tasks.

The second dimension of children's growth as writers is what they say. It is particularly important to look for evidence that children are learning to organize their writing better, to develop their ideas more fully, and to use features that are associated with written language rather than oral language (Once upon a time…).

However, a word of warning is in order. As children begin to use more sophisticated writing strategies (in particular, as they concentrate on developmental spellings), the content and organization of their stories and journal entries may appear to become less sophisticated for a period of time. Rather than being taken as a cause for alarm, this state of affairs should be viewed as more of a natural trade-off. When children do get more control over sound-symbol relationships, they will again be able to attend more closely to what it is they want to say and to whom they want to say it.

4.

Copying Environmental Print

5.

Early Developmental Spelling

Early Developmental Spelling

φ W + C D p d B

Finally, it is important to remember that children's reading and writing development are integrally related, and this reading/writing connection must be taken into account in evaluating their growth as writers.

In particular, as a child reads what he or she has written, it is important to ask questions such as these:

- Does the child attend to the picture or the print in reading what she or he has written?

- Are the child's attempts to track the print successful?

- Does the child conventionally read what he or she has written?

- Does the child's intonation sound more like oral or written language?

As children move along the developmental pathway, their rereadings of their own writing become more print-based and sound increasingly like written language rather than oral language.

5.

Full Developmental Spelling

I lik ron Bos Be kus tha
r Color fool

Andrew

5.

Transitional Spelling

5-2-85

Andrew

I llKe CooKes And
Caks And I theK
I Know To Mak theeM
uoos flan Wet And egg

6.

STUDENTS ACQUIRING ENGLISH

EMERGENT LITERACY IN THE SECOND LANGUAGE

BY JOSEFINA VILLAMIL TINAJERO

The early childhood years are a remarkably active period for acquiring language and for learning about its written form. Classroom environments have a significant effect on children's language and literacy development. This is especially true for emergent readers and writers who are also acquiring English as a second language. The physical and social environment of the classroom, teacher beliefs and attitudes about language acquisition and emergent literacy, the types of activities planned, and the strategies and techniques used by teachers all affect the opportunities children have to emerge as readers and writers and to acquire a new language.

Supporting Kindergartners' Language Acquisition

It is our position that children *acquire* rather than *learn* a language in a natural progression of stages. As language is acquired, literacy in the new language develops. That is, current research suggests that the second language is acquired in the same manner as the first and that it is acquired most effectively in a highly interactive, total communication environment.

Children acquire language when they understand what people say to them or what is read. They acquire language by understanding messages and by responding to those messages in meaningful ways. Language must make sense to young children, and somehow it must be important for them to acquire it. Some of the best ways to encourage language development are to provide children with many opportunities to interact with other children, to encourage child's play, and to engage them in natural language activities. Songs, poems, stories, games, role-play, story theater, and dramatizations are especially effective because they allow students to hear natural English while providing a meaningful, motivating, and enjoyable context for learning.

Young SAEs need a favorable environment for language acquisition, an environment that is as natural and as language-rich as that within which they learned their first language. Kindergartners acquiring English, in particular, need many opportunities to hear and use English, to experiment with it, to take risks and try out their knowledge of the language. They need to be encouraged to express their ideas and feelings as they move along the pathway toward nativelike fluency.

When students offer responses, for example, their pronunciation may be poor and their grammatical construction may include elements from their first language. When this happens, teachers need to accept their responses, model the "correct" form in a tactful and unexaggerated way, and praise them for their contributions. Praising builds confidence and helps children feel valued as members of the class. They will also be much more motivated to "experiment" with the language and to take risks—that is, express their thoughts and ideas even if they are not yet fully fluent in the language.

Teachers can integrate the following techniques with activities planned for other children in the class.

Heterogeneous Grouping. One way to provide SAEs with opportunities to practice their English is to increase the frequency and variety of interactions among students. Pairing them with proficient English speakers for activities such as partner "reading" of Big Books and partner story retellings is one way of increasing interaction. Grouping them with students of varying proficiencies for activities such as illustrating a new ending to a story or illustrating a character map is another. At other times, however, SAEs may be grouped together for activities such as listening to a story in their native language, working on a special project, or doing partner reading with other SAEs.

Cooperative Learning. Cooperative learning also increases the frequency and variety of second language practice through different types of interactions. It provides students with many opportunities to utilize newly acquired language and to "read and write" (scribbling and drawing are considered writing at this age) in English in a "safe" social situation where they don't feel threatened by error correction. Cooperative learning also provides students with opportunities to act as resources for each other and thus assume a more active role in learning.

When working with kindergartners acquiring English, it is also important to keep in mind that, as individuals, they are at different levels of English proficiency. Thus, when planning activities for them, teachers must be aware of the level of receptive and productive language they bring to the learning task. There may be some children who may not be ready to begin producing oral English. Some may be experiencing what is often referred to as the *"silent period" of language learning*. That is, second language learners go through a period of time during which they prefer to listen rather than to produce language. As with most second language learners, children's receptive

language skills develop earlier than their productive ones (Rice, 1989).

It is important, however, to keep in mind that language learning is taking place during this time (Evans, 1990). Children don't always need to respond in order to learn new language skills. They can benefit greatly from the opportunity to absorb the conversations of others (Rice, 1989).

𝒰sing Literature to Nurture Children's Language Development

The best language lessons are good books and interesting discussions in which children are absorbed in the meaning of what is said to them or what is read.

For SAEs, literature cultivates language, provides language models, and facilitates language acquisition. As children listen to rhymes, poems, and patterned/predictable stories in English, they learn new language patterns and idiomatic usages, which are assimilated as children apply them to express their own thoughts and ideas during meaningful, well-planned lessons. Children with limited vocabulary can latch on to the "new" language they have heard, suddenly discovering that their former limited vocabulary takes on new dimensions.

𝒮torytelling with SAEs

Because storytelling encourages physical, visual, and aural/oral participation of students, it is an excellent context for teaching language and concepts to SAEs.

Listening and speaking skills, for example, are enriched through the use of puppetry, tapes, dramatic presentations, and the teacher's systematic reading to children. Children will also enjoy retelling stories they have been told or sharing stories from their own cultures, stories they may have learned at home or in their neighborhoods. Children's own creativity and ingenuity can also be encouraged and supported by allowing children to create, tell, and retell their own stories.

Following are some suggestions to take full advantage of storytelling activities to enhance language development for SAEs.

Oral Previewing. This technique adjusts the teacher's language input to children's language proficiency and comprehension level during storytelling. For SAEs, oral previewing takes the form of paraphrasing or telling the story "in your own words," both to make the story as comprehensible as possible and to facilitate language development. When using this technique, follow these guidelines.

First, screen the story, taking into account the language and experiential knowledge of students. Select areas of difficulty such as idiomatic language and difficult vocabulary. Become familiar with the story so that the retelling is as natural as possible, and so that you can be cognizant of facial expressions that might indicate whether or not SAEs are understanding the story.

Then hold up a copy of the book as you lead the children orally through the story, establishing plot and setting. Use gestures, body language, and facial expressions to help convey ideas and

Students Acquiring English

concepts. Use simple, well-formed sentences; limit sentence length and complexity while maintaining appropriate grammar and intonation.

Clarify the meaning of words, phrases, and idiomatic expressions using context clues, such as pointing to the illustrations or drawing simple pictures. Make frequent repetitions of key words and ideas. At times, incorporate role play to help children understand concepts and learn language through physical activity.

As you continue to go through the story, ask questions that require yes/no responses, a nod of the head, pointing to an illustration, or one- or two-word responses to check understanding. Also ask questions to relate the story situation to children's experiences. Remember that SAEs understand more than they can verbalize. As children respond using one or two words, repeat their utterances, use their words in an expanded comment. That is, use the *semantic expansion* technique, in which you as the teacher start with something the child said and elaborate to clarify or add to the response. Also, use structural expansion in which you as the teacher repeat an incorrect utterance correctly to model for the children. Finally, have children make predictions along the way to encourage language use and development of critical thinking skills. Remember to praise children for their contributions.

These types of teacher-child interactions with storybooks create a context for comprehending meaning, for making meaning. They help SAEs get past some of the difficult language so they can concentrate on the story line. Children also internalize new language related to the story they are about to hear.

The following storytelling variations help SAEs acquire language and make stories more comprehensible. Use them as often as possible. They are good for all children.

Puppetry. Puppets make stories come alive for children, and the actions associated with using them to tell or retell stories make language more comprehensible. Most important, however, SAEs are less reluctant to talk "when they take on other identities to perform. It is somehow less threatening to make a mistake as someone else; it becomes their mistake, not that of the student" (Evans, 1990).

Participation Stories. Certain stories invite children to participate actively as they respond to certain words that act as cues for actions like clapping or stamping their feet or shaking their heads. Before reading the story, the teacher introduces the cues. The children then act out the story as the teacher reads. These types of stories develop listening skills and facilitate language acquisition (Evans, 1990).

Pantomime. Through pantomime children use their whole bodies for making meaning as they participate in storytelling activities. Text becomes more comprehensible as characters come alive.

Story Retelling. Working with a partner, children retell stories to one another. Story retelling provides a great opportunity for children to use the language they have heard in the stories to express their own thoughts and ideas.

Tape Recordings. Tape recordings of stories are an excellent way to expose students to good literature that may be beyond their reading abilities but within their listening abilities. Children will also enjoy making their own recordings of

stories. These recordings also serve as good diagnostic tools.

Choral Reading. Choral readings of stories, with a mix of SAEs and proficient English speakers, give shy learners a safe way to practice formal speaking. Remember, the desire of SAEs to produce language varies greatly—allow them to join in when they're ready.

Shared Reading and SAEs

Another excellent way to provide SAEs with rich literature experiences is to conduct shared reading with books that contain repetitive language and/or predictable outcomes. The repetitive characteristics of the texts facilitate the natural acquisition of vocabulary, pronunciation, and language structures. Big Books are particularly effective for group study and for exposing children to print.

The repeated readings help children to read more efficiently, gain confidence, practice using their reading skills, and increase their sight vocabulary. And since the illustrations in the books are closely tied to the text, children get visual support for the rapid development of a wide range of vocabulary. The reading and rereading of stories also allow SAEs to hear and practice, in an informal setting, the rhythm and structure of English.

As children recite and participate in shared reading activities using rhymes, poems, songs, and pattern stories, they learn new language patterns. They internalize these patterns and then use them to express their own thoughts and ideas. Furthermore, through shared reading, children are exposed to the written and oral forms of language and are offered numerous opportunities to develop listening, speaking, reading, and writing skills at the "teachable moment."

Shared reading activities also establish the kind of low-anxiety environment essential to language acquisition and provide SAEs at varying/lower levels of English proficiency with the opportunity to participate with the rest of the class. It is also a pleasurable experience that helps SAEs develop a positive attitude toward acquiring English and learning to read in a second language.

In selecting materials to use with SAEs, select those with texts containing features such as rhyme, rhythmic language, predictable or repetitive plots and language patterns, or illustrations that closely parallel the text. Screen materials carefully for overload of idiomatic language and situations that are culturally unfamiliar. Finally, select materials at the appropriate instructional level that foster students' appreciation of reading and develop positive attitudes toward learning to read in English.

Language Experience Activities

The language experience approach is particularly suitable for use with SAEs because the children's language proficiency, no matter how limited, is valued and used as a starting point for further development. And because SAEs' proficiency in English often varies significantly, language experience activities help build a common knowledge and language base for them. The approach also integrates children's ideas, interests, experiences, and natural language, using them to motivate students to read.

Through language experience, SAEs are also able to acquire the basic skills of reading and writing with familiar material—their own. Thus, the text is rich in comprehensible content that further develops children's language proficiency.

Establishing Partnerships with Parents

A primary way in which we can provide more supportive learning environments for all children is to involve their parents, working with them as colleagues, inviting them to participate as valuable resources of information and perspectives, and sharing with them ways in which parents enhance education at home.

Parents can assist teachers in creating more supportive and nurturing learning environments that offer the security needed for SAEs to participate in a culturally different setting. Parents can be invited to the classroom to tell stories from the oral tradition, to read stories, read or recite poetry, share "how to" information, and present topics that have inspired and informed their lives.

Parents often think that they cannot help their children at home if they do not speak English. Teachers need to make an effort to assure them that working with their children in their native language is of benefit because concepts learned in the native language will transfer to English.

The Challenge

Kindergarten is a critical point for students acquiring English. Beyond their

needs for skills in academic growth, SAEs also have motivational and emotional needs that must be met. These needs are often magnified in importance where there are cultural and linguistic differences between the school and the home. They include children's need to feel a sense of identity, to belong, to be understood by and communicate with significant others, and to succeed in environments in which they are accepted and respected. Kindergarten teachers can make a difference in the lives of these children. By simply applying some of the basic principles discussed here, teachers can provide a nurturing and intellectually stimulating environment where students acquiring English can succeed and thrive.

References

Auerbach, E. (1989). Toward a social-contextual approach to family literacy. Harvard Educational Review, 59, No. 2, pp. 165–181.

Early, M. (1991). Using wordless picture books to promote second language learning. ELT Journal. Volume 45/3. July. pp. 245–250.

Evans, L. S. (1990). Storytelling and oral language development in ESL classrooms. TESOL Newsletter. October. pp. 3, 16, 18, 30.

Flood, J.; Lapp, D.; Tinajero, J.; and Nagel, G. Parents and teachers: Partners in developing literacy for multicultural students. (unpublished manuscript).

Nurss, J. R. and Hough, R. A. (1985). Story reading: Language arts for limited English speakers. TESOL Newsletter. Vol. 8, No. 1. pp. 1–2.

Rice, M. (1989). Children's language acquisition. American Psychologist. Volume 4. February. pp. 149–156.

INTRODUCING SING AND DANCE AWAY!

Invite children to explore singing and dancing through trade books, read aloud selections, poetry, and songs!

TRADE BOOKS

Oh, A-Hunting We Will Go
by *John Langstaff,*
pictures by Nancy Winslow Parker
These captured animals are put in some silly positions before they are let go! Available as a Big Book and little book, and included on the
LISTENING LIBRARY AUDIOCASSETTE

Max
by *Rachel Isadora*
When Max's sister invites him to her dance class, Max discovers that ballet can be as challenging and fun as baseball!

The Little Band
by *James Sage,*
illustrated by Keiko Narahashi
A band marches through a town and changes it forever.

READ ALOUDS

TEACHER'S READ ALOUD ANTHOLOGY
Twelve Dancing Princesses
A *Brothers Grimm fairy tale*
retold by Margaret H. Lippert
A poor soldier helps a king solve the mystery of where the King's daughters dance all night.

The Clever Turtle
A *Hispanic folk tale retold by Margaret H. Lippert*
A turtle outsmarts a family that is planning to make it into turtle soup.

BIG BOOKS

BIG BOOK OF POEMS
Singing-Time
by Rose Fyleman

BIG BOOK OF SONGS
You'll Sing a Song and I'll Sing a Song
by Ella Jenkins

Also Available—

SING & READ BOOKS AND AUDIOCASSETTES
You'll Sing a Song and I'll Sing a Song

SONGS AND STORIES AUDIOCASSETTES
Story Songs—including the
Theme Song—and Storytellings

EXPLORING PRINT

BIG BOOK OF ALPHABET RHYMES AND CHIMES
PLUS RHYME AND CHIME STRIPS

• **Hh** Hippity Hop to Bed

• **Mm** Miss Mary Mack

Also Available—

SING A SOUND AUDIOCASSETTES
Songs for language play and
for developing
phonemic awareness!

THEME 5: SING AND DANCE AWAY!
Overview for Week 1

LITERATURE	SHARING TIME	READING AND WRITING
1 THEME POEM "Singing-Time"	**Today's News** and talking about songs and dances p. 35	Reading and Reciting the Theme Poem and Responding through **Poem Talk** and Journal Writing pp. 36-37
2 OH, A-HUNTING WE WILL GO	**Today's News** and playing "Hunter's Tag" p. 43	Reading *Oh, A-Hunting We Will Go* and Responding through **Book Talk**, Journal Writing, and Story Theater pp. 44-45
3 OH, A-HUNTING WE WILL GO	**Today's News** and playing a game while singing "Oh, A-Hunting We Will Go" p. 49	Rereading *Oh, A-Hunting We Will Go* and Responding through **Book Talk**, Making a Class Big Book, and Performing the Song pp. 50-51
4 MAX	**Today's News** and dancing to music p. 55	Reading *Max* and Responding through **Book Talk**, Journal Writing, and Story Theater pp. 56-57
5 MAX	**Today's News** and reading the poem "Don't Dress Your Cat in an Apron" p. 61	Rereading *Max* and Responding through **Book Talk,** Writing About Baseball or Ballet, and Dramatizing the Story pp. 62-63

THEME WORDS: SINGER, DANCER

Each theme helps children see themselves from a different perspective. This theme helps children see themselves as *singers* and *dancers.*

EXPLORING PRINT

Decoding and Phonics
Letters *H, h*
Sound/Letter Relationships /h/ *H, h*
SONG: "Hambone"
pp. 46-47

Decoding and Phonics
Letters *H, h*
Sound/Letter Relationships /h/ *H, h*
BIG BOOK OF ALPHABET RHYMES AND CHIMES:
"Hippity Hop to Bed"
pp. 52-53

Concepts of Print
Directionality, Words
RHYME AND CHIME STRIPS:
"Hippity Hop to Bed"
pp. 58-59

Decoding and Phonics
Letters *H, h*
Sound/Letter Relationships /h/ *H, h*
Concepts of Print
Directionality, Words, Letters
RHYME AND CHIME STRIPS:
"Hippity Hop to Bed"
pp. 64-65

THEME GOALS AND OUTCOMES

The literature and activities in this theme were carefully selected and reviewed by the program authors and by the multicultural, literature, and educational consultants who worked together to develop the program goals and outcomes.

MULTICULTURAL PERSPECTIVES

Appreciate and value diverse points of view

Become aware of cultural backgrounds, experiences, emotions, and ideas of self and others through literature

Appreciate the literary expression of our contemporary multicultural society and multicultural heritage

Appreciate the universality of literary themes in many cultures and in many different times

Appreciate the significance of traditional literature within a culture

Recognize cultural attitudes and customs in literary selections

PERSONAL INTERESTS AND ATTITUDES

Develop an awareness of the classroom as a community of learners that values cooperation, fair play, and respect for others and for oneself

Select stories and books for personal interests

Develop personal reading and writing interests

Make connections between one's personal life and literature

Choose to read and write for a variety of purposes

Share, review, and recommend books to others

Participate in reading, writing, listening, and viewing activities

Appreciate the artistic interpretation of literature through film, illustration, photography, dance, oral presentations, and other forms of expression

THEME 5: SING AND DANCE AWAY!
Overview for Week 2

LITERATURE	SHARING TIME	READING AND WRITING
6 **READ ALOUD** "The Twelve Dancing Princesses"	**Today's News** and dancing to "Dancin' to the Beat" p. 67	Reading "The Twelve Dancing Princesses" and Responding through **Book Talk**, Making a Story Mural, and Story Theater pp. 68-69
7 *THE LITTLE BAND*	**Today's News** and singing "The Finger Band" p. 73	Reading *The Little Band* and Responding through **Book Talk**, Journal Writing, and Making a Story Mural pp. 74-75
8 *THE LITTLE BAND*	**Today's News** and singing "Parade Came Marching" p. 79	Rereading *The Little Band* and Responding through **Book Talk**, Writing Newspaper Articles, and Story Theater pp. 80-81
9 **READ ALOUD** "The Clever Turtle"	**Today's News** and singing and dancing to "Sambalele" p. 85	Reading "The Clever Turtle" and Responding through **Book Talk**, Journal Writing, and Diorama Performances pp. 86-87
10 *OH, A-HUNTING WE WILL GO* *MAX* *THE LITTLE BAND*	**Today's News** and rereading the Theme Poem "Singing-Time" and singing the Theme Song "You'll Sing a Song and I'll Sing a Song" p. 91	Reviewing the theme trade books and Responding through **Book Talk** and Journal Writing pp. 92-93

Exploring Print

Integrating Language Arts and Other Curriculum Areas

Into the Learning Centers!

Mᴏʀᴇ Bᴏᴏᴋs ᴛᴏ Sʜᴀʀᴇ

The books on these pages can be shared with children throughout the theme. The books can also be put into the Reading Center so children can read and enjoy them.

Mᴏʀᴇ ʙᴏᴏᴋs ᴀʙᴏᴜᴛ sɪɴɢɪɴɢ ᴀɴᴅ ᴅᴀɴᴄɪɴɢ

■ **SONG AND DANCE MAN**
by Karen Ackerman, illus. by Stephen Gammell (Knopf, 1988). The best part about visiting Grandpa is watching him recreate his old vaudeville song and dance act complete with tap shoes, banjo, and magic tricks.

■ **GRANDMA'S BAND**
by Brad Bowles, illus. by Anthony Chan (Stemmer House, 1989). Grandma discovers one morning (and so will your kindergartners) that a washboard and various pots and pans make fine instruments for an impromptu band.

■ **WHEN BLUEBELL SANG**
by Lisa Campbell Ernst (Bradbury, 1989). All over the country people flock to hear Bluebell, a most amazing singing cow. Although Bluebell and Farmer Swenson soon tire of show biz, their greedy agent will not allow them to return home. Then Bluebell hatches a perfect plan. . . .

■ **WHALE SONG**
by Tony Johnston, illus. by Ed Young (G. P. Putnam's Sons, 1987). Magnificently illustrated by Caldecott Award winner Ed Young, this counting book lyrically celebrates the beauty of these giants of the sea.

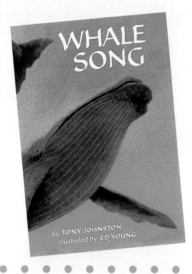

■ **MUSICAL MAX**
by Robert Kraus, illus. by Jose Aruego and Ariane Dewey (Simon and Schuster, 1990). In this delightful book by an illustrious author/illustrator team, Max's family and neighbors discover that music really does make life more harmonious.

■ **GOING TO MY BALLET CLASS**
by Susan Kuklin (Bradbury, 1989). The lively text narrated by a young dancer and the full-color photographs give the reader an inside look at a beginning dance class at the Joffrey Ballet School.

■ **THE FLUTE PLAYER: AN APACHE FOLK TALK**
retold by Michael Lacapa (Northland, 1990). Some say they hear the wind blowing in the canyon, but Michael Lacapa, remembering the traditions of his people, knows that it is the sorrowful sound made by a flute player, mourning the loss of his loved one.

■ **BARN DANCE**
by Bill Martin, Jr. and John Archambault, illus. by Ted Rand (Holt, 1986). "There's magic in the air," says the owl as he calls the animals to the rollicking barn dance. The rhymed text and luminous illustrations heighten the reader's sense of fantasy.

■ NICHOLAS CRICKET

by Joyce Maxner, illus. by William Joyce (Harper Trophy, 1989). A wonderful read aloud selection. The rhyming text imitates musical rhythms as the Bug-a-Wug Cricket Band plays far into the night.

■ ABIYOYO

by Pete Seeger, illus. by Michael Hays (Macmillan, 1986). In this elaboration by Pete Seeger on a South African folk tale, a young boy and his father use music to save their town from the dreaded giant.

■ DANCE AWAY

by George Shannon, illus. by Jose Aruego and Ariane Dewey (Mulberry, 1991). Rabbit's friends are annoyed by his constant dancing. They change their minds, however, when, about to become dinner for Fox, Rabbit dances them safely away.

■ WHEELS ON THE BUS

illus. by Sylvie Kantorovitz Wickstrom (Crown, 1988). A "Raffi Songs to Read" book. The lively illustrations deftly capture the mood of this familiar song. The music reproduced on the last page should encourage readers to burst into song.

■ MUSIC, MUSIC FOR EVERYONE

by Vera B. Williams (Mulberry, 1984). When Grandma becomes ill, Rosa and her friends play music to cheer her up. Soon the whole neighborhood is dancing to their music as the children raise money to help pay Grandma's expenses.

MORE BOOKS BY THEME AUTHORS AND ILLUSTRATORS

■ AT THE CROSSROADS

by Rachel Isadora (Greenwillow, 1991). The author/illustrator's watercolors vividly capture the South African landscape as she describes the joyful expectation of a group of children who patiently await their fathers' return after months of working in the distant mines.

■ OVER IN THE MEADOW

by John Langstaff, illus. by Feodor Rojankovsky (HBJ, 1985). Langstaff and Rojankovsky won the Caldecott Medal for their previous collaboration, *Frog Went A-Courtin'*. Children will delight in this book as they pore over the illustrations and sing the amusing verses.

■ I HAVE A FRIEND

by Keiko Narahashi (Margaret K. McElderry Books, 1987). Brillantly colored watercolors and a poetic text portray a small boy's friend—his shadow—who arrives with the sun but leaves each evening at dusk.

■ TO SLEEP

by James Sage, illus. by Warwick Hutton (Margaret K. McElderry Books, 1990). A young child tries to prolong the moment when he must go to bed. His mother's gentle and imaginative responses finally lull him to sleep.

1
SING AND DANCE AWAY!

LITERATURE

Big Book of Poems: Singing Time
   by Rose Fyleman

Big Book of Songs: You'll Sing a
Song and I'll Sing a Song
   by Ella Jenkins

 SONGS AND STORIES
AUDIOCASSETTES STORY SONGS:
You'll Sing a Song and I'll Sing a Song
STORY SONGS: Mi Cuerpo Hace Musica

 SING & READ BOOKS AND
AUDIOCASSETTES
You'll Sing a Song and I'll Sing a Song

EXPLORING PRINT

Literature Activity Book: pp. 42–43
   Sing and Dance Away!

STAFF DEVELOPMENT A to EZ Handbook:

- Journals: p. 264

- Music and Movement: p. 274

Performance Assessment Handbook
HomeWords: Home-School Resources

OTHER RESOURCES

- BIG BOOK STAND
- BIG BOOK POINTER
- CHART PAPER
- MARKERS

LITERACY SUPPORT:
*B*UILDING LANGUAGE
AND CONCEPTS

**For children acquiring English and/or
needing more intensive support, you
may wish to incorporate the following
suggestions into the basic lesson plan.**

Involve the class in a singing and dancing activity such as the
"Hokey Pokey" song. Encourage children to dance in their own
unique style as they sing the words, "you do the hokey pokey
and you turn yourself around." Afterwards, ask children to
share what part of the activity they liked best.

Sharing Time

TODAY'S NEWS

Gather children together and write and read Today's News, running your hand under the words as you read.

Are you a singer or a dancer? Today we will all be singers!

CREATING INTEREST AND BUILDING BACKGROUND

Because motivation matters!

Introduce the theme SING AND DANCE AWAY! by asking children to name their favorite songs. List these on a chart and keep the chart on display throughout the theme to add children's suggestions.

OUR FAVORITE SONGS

Old MacDonald
The Wheels on the Bus

Ask children to tell about their experiences dancing. Encourage them to use a form of the word *dance* when they describe these experiences. For example, *I danced with my brother at my cousin's wedding.*

Point to the words *singer* and *dancer*. Share that the Theme Words are *singer* and *dancer*. Talk about how the words are connected and how some singers are also dancers. Invite children to be singers and dancers throughout this theme!

Reading and Writing

Sharing Literature
"Singing-Time"

LISTEN TO THE SOUNDS OF POETRY Invite children to listen to the Theme Poem "Singing-Time." Practice reading the poem ahead of time so you can capture its lilting quality.

Reread the poem, asking children what the first thing they do in the morning is. Then invite them to say the poem with you. The short length and simple rhyme pattern of "Singing-Time" make it ideal for choral reading.

SEE THE POEM IN PRINT Display the Theme Poem "Singing-Time" on pages 18–19 in the *Big Book of Poems.* Explain that the poem children have been listening to and reciting is the poem they can see in the Big Book.

Read the poem again, tracking the print with the Big Book pointer.

Singing-Time

I wake in the morning early
And always, the very first thing,
I poke out my head and I sit up in bed
And I sing and I sing and I sing.

Rose Fyleman

Big Book of Poems, pages 18–19

RESPONDING TO LITERATURE

POEM TALK Encourage children to share personal responses to the poem. You may want to begin by sharing your reaction to provide a model for personal involvement with literature.

Build on this sharing of responses with a discussion of the poem. You may want to present some of the prompts below to get the discussion started.

- *How do you wake up in the morning? Do you listen to a song? Do you sing?*

- *Does anyone wake you up in the morning by singing? What do they sing?*

JOURNAL WRITING Provide theme journals for children to personalize by stapling approximately ten sheets of paper together or have children bring in journals to use.

Invite children to refer to the chart of Our Favorite Songs and to add other favorite songs they may have thought of. Then ask them to write about their favorite "waking up" song.

As children write, model writing in your own journal, perhaps by choosing a favorite song and writing about why you like to sing it or hear it being sung.

After writing, ask children if they would like to share what they wrote with the group.

Team Work/Theme Work — A Song and Dance Concert!

Introducing the Project: Come Hear Us Sing! Come See Us Dance!

Generate excitement for putting together a Song and Dance Concert by inviting children to talk about what a concert is, why people go to concerts, and what kinds of songs and dances can be performed. Then ask them to offer ideas about how they could produce a concert for family and friends.

Brainstorming and Sharing Ideas

Ask children to name songs that they know and dances that they know how to do. List their responses on chart paper. Invite volunteers to sing songs they know and to demonstrate dances they know. You may want to teach children to sing and dance to the three songs on pages 40–41.

SONGS WE KNOW	DANCES WE KNOW
The Farmer in the Dell	The Hokey-Pokey
Old MacDonald	London Bridge
Eency, Weency Spider	Ring Around a' Rosies
Twinkle, Twinkle, Little Star	
The Mulberry Bush	
Row, Row, Row Your Boat	

Ask children to suggest tasks that need to be done to make the concert a success and list their ideas on a chart. Read the chart to children, pointing to each word as you read it.

Practice songs and dances
Write invitations
Make costumes
Make a welcome poster

Explain to children that as they work on the project, they will be able to learn new songs and dances and choose which ones they wish to perform in the concert.

Sing Out!

To get children in a performing mood, have them sing the Theme Song, "You'll Sing a Song and I'll Sing a Song" on pages 16–17 in the *Big Book of Songs.* Play the song on the STORY SONGS AUDIOCASSETTE a few times until children feel comfortable singing along. Point to the words of the song with the Big Book pointer as children sing. Encourage children to dance along to the song if they wish.

Planning

As you work through the theme with children, add songs and dances that children learn to the chart. Set aside time each day for children to practice their singing and dancing in preparation for the Song and Dance Concert. Children may want to use the instruments they make in the Learning Centers to accompany a song or dance. (See page 103.)

Encourage children to work together to decide who will perform what song or dance in the concert, and in what order. Once the concert plan is in place, ask children to decide whom they wish to invite to their concert. Challenge them to create invitations and posters announcing the concert.

♪ SONGS AND STORIES AUDIOCASSETTE
STORY SONGS: You'll Sing a Song and I'll Sing a Song

You'll Sing a Song

You'll sing a song,
And I'll sing a song,
And we'll sing a song
together.

and I'll Sing a Song

You'll sing a song,
And I'll sing a song,
In warm or wintry weather.
In warm or wintry weather.

Ella Jenkins

Big Book of Songs, pages 16–17

TEAM WORK/THEME WORK   A SONG AND DANCE CONCERT!

Old Brass Wagon

Circle to the left, old brass wagon;
Circle to the left, old brass wagon;
Circle to the left, old brass wagon;
You're the one my darling.

Children join hands and circle left.

Circle to the right, old brass wagon;
Circle to the right, old brass wagon;
Circle to the right, old brass wagon;
You're the one my darling.

Children join hands and circle right.

Everybody in, old brass wagon;
Everybody in, old brass wagon;
Everybody in, old brass wagon;
You're the one my darling.

Children walk to center of circle, swinging hands forward and up.

Everybody out, old brass wagon;
Everybody out, old brass wagon;
Everybody out, old brass wagon;
You're the one my darling.

Children walk backwards, extending hands to the rear.

You may wish to teach one or all of these songs to children. Copy the songs onto chart paper and display them throughout the theme. Point to each word with your finger or the Big Book pointer as you sing or read the words. Remind children to practice singing and dancing to these songs if they wish to include them in their Song and Dance concert.

Developing Multicultural Awareness

Tinga Layo

Chorus
Tinga Layo! Come, little donkey, come;
Tinga Layo! Come, little donkey, come.

Use hands to imitate donkey ears.

My donkey walk, my donkey talk,
My donkey eat with a knife and fork;
My donkey walk, my donkey talk,
My donkey eat with a knife and fork.

Make finger motions to show walking and talking on appropriate lines. Pantomime eating with knife and fork.

Chorus
My donkey eat, my donkey sleep,
My donkey kick with his two hind feet;
My donkey eat, my donkey sleep,
My donkey kick with his two hind feet.

Pantomime eating and sleeping. Kick one leg back at a time to imitate donkey kicking.

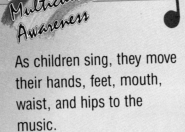

Mi Cuerpo Hace Musica

Mi cuerpo, mi cuerpo hace musica.
Mi cuerpo, mi cuerpo hace musica.
Mis manos hacen pom, pom, pom.
Mis pies hacen bom, bom, bom.
Mi boca hace la, la, la.
Cintura hace cha, cha, cha,
Cha, cha, cha.

Mi cuerpo, mi cuerpo hace musica.
Mi cuerpo, mi cuerpo hace musica.
My hands say pom, pom, pom.
My feet say bom, bom, bom.
My mouth says la, la, la.
My waist says cha, cha, cha,
Cha, cha, cha.

There's music, there's music,
   there's music inside me.
There's music, there's music,
   there's music inside me.
Mis manos hacen pom, pom, pom.
Mis pies hacen bom, bom, bom.
Mi boca hace la, la, la.
Cintura hace cha, cha, cha.

Cha, cha, cha, cha, cha, cha.
My waist and hips say cha, cha, cha.
La, la, la, la, la, la.
My mouth says la, la, la.
Bom, bom, bom, bom, bom, bom.
My feet say bom, bom, bom.
Pom, pom, pom, pom, pom, pom.
My hands say pom, pom, pom.

Mi cuerpo, mi cuerpo hace musica.
Mi cuerpo, mi cuerpo hace musica.
There's music inside me!

   —Sarah Pirtle's version of the
   traditional song

As children sing, they move their hands, feet, mouth, waist, and hips to the music.

INTO THE LEARNING CENTERS
You may wish to place the Sing & Read Book and its audiocassette for "You'll Sing a Song and I'll Sing a Song" in the Reading Center and invite children to listen to the tape as they read the book. See page 98.

2
SING AND DANCE AWAY!

LITERATURE

Oh, A-Hunting We Will Go
by John Langstaff,
illustrated by
Nancy Winslow Parker

LISTENING LIBRARY
AUDIOCASSETTES
Oh, A-Hunting We Will Go

SING & READ BOOKS AND
AUDIOCASSETTES
You'll Sing a Song
and I'll Sing a Song

EXPLORING PRINT

SING A SOUND AUDIOCASSETTES
Hambone

Learning the Code: H, h

Practice Book: p. 13

BRWL: Letterbook H(12)

STAFF DEVELOPMENT

A to EZ Handbook
• Big Books: p. 246
• Shared Reading: p. 299

Performance Assessment Handbook

OTHER RESOURCES

• BIG BOOK STAND
• BIG BOOK POINTER
• CHART PAPER
• MARKERS
• TO MAKE JOURNALS
   STAPLER
   UNLINED PAPER
   CONSTRUCTION
     PAPER

LITERACY SUPPORT:
Building Language and Concepts

For children acquiring English and/or needing more intensive support, you may wish to incorporate the following suggestions into the basic lesson plan.

Before reading the selection, define the word *hunting* for children. Explain how hunting animals for fun has made some beautiful animals become "extinct" or "endangered." Tell children that in this story/song the boys and girls pretend to hunt the animals but they always let them go free.

SHARING TIME

TODAY'S NEWS

As you read and write Today's News, point to the words. Ask children to name the words that rhyme.

A story song!
A story song!
Today we'll sing one loud and strong.

CREATING INTEREST AND BUILDING BACKGROUND

Because motivation matters!

To prepare children for the story and song *Oh, A-Hunting We Will Go,* a story about an imaginary hunt, play a version of "Freeze Tag" called "Hunter's Tag."

- Divide children into groups of four with one child as the hunter and the other three as the animals.

- The hunter tries to tag the animals, who must freeze when touched.

- The animals can unfreeze each other with a tap on the shoulder.

Introduce children to the song "Oh, A-Hunting We Will Go." You may want to copy the first verse of the song on chart paper and display it in the Reading or Writing Center.

Oh, A-Hunting We Will Go

Oh, a-hunting we will go,
A-hunting we will go;
We'll catch a fox
    and put him in a box,
And then we'll let him go!

READING AND WRITING

SHARING LITERATURE
Oh, A-Hunting We Will Go

LOOK IT OVER   Display the Big Book for *Oh, A-Hunting We Will Go.* Explain that the Big Book lets everyone see the words and pictures in the book. Place the little book version in the Reading Center for children to explore on their own. Hold up the cover of *Oh, A-Hunting We Will Go,* reading the words of the title, pointing to them as you read. Point to the author's name, John Langstaff, and the illustrator's name, Nancy Winslow Parker.

Talk with children about what they notice on the cover. Open the book to display both front and back covers simultaneously so children can make predictions about who the hunters are and what animals they will sing about.

Make a prediction chart to record children's ideas. Review the predictions children have made after you have read the story with them.

What Animals Will We Sing About?

snake — Peter
bear — Bob
pig — Maria

Share the author's dedication, "For all the children who helped me make up extra verses for this folk song." Tell children that they too will make up extra verses during this theme.

SHARE THE STORY   As you read, point to and emphasize the rhyming words in each verse. Take time to show the details of the illustrations.

About the Author and Illustrator

Share with children that John Langstaff is a storyteller and musician who attended a choir school when he was eight years old, where he learned to sing. He has worked as a concert singer, teacher, and Artistic Director of *Young Audiences* in Boston, Massachusetts. Langstaff has been the producer of *The Revels,* a production that involves singing and dancing. He continues to involve children of all ages in musical experiences.

Point to Nancy Winslow Parker's name and tell children that she has illustrated many books, including *The Goat in the Rug.* She has been drawing since she was in kindergarten and loves drawing animals more than anything else.

RESPONDING TO LITERATURE

BOOK TALK   Invite children to share their personal reactions to the book. You may want to present some of the prompts below to get the discussion started, or you may want to talk about your reactions to the book and the parts you found funny.

- *Which rhymes did you like the best?*

- *Which rhymes made you laugh?*

- *Looking at the illustrations helped me figure out that* pram *is another word for a "baby carriage." How did the illustrations help you?*

JOURNAL WRITING   Invite children to write and draw about their favorite rhymes. Join children by writing in your journal at the same time. Ask children if they would like to share what they wrote with the group.

STORY THEATER   Listen to the story of "Oh, A-Hunting We Will Go" on the LISTENING LIBRARY AUDIOCASSETTE together, inviting children to join in. Then play the audiocassette again and invite children to pantomime the action in the book.

TEAM WORK/THEME WORK
Set aside time for children to practice singing "Oh, A-Hunting We Will Go" if they wish to include it in the Song and Dance Concert. See pages 38–41 and 94–95.

INTO THE LEARNING CENTERS
Today would be a good day to direct children to the Games Center where they can play the game Oh, A-Hunting We Will Go. See page 105.

While writing her journal entry, Rebecca devoted considerable attention to pulling apart the sounds within the words she was writing and to deciding which letters to use to represent those sounds.
Rebecca read her message like this: "I think the book was funny."

EXPLORING PRINT LEARNING THE CODE

In the Exploring Print lessons for this theme, children will learn about the letters H, h and M, m and the sounds they represent. Take advantage of opportunities to point out these letters and the sounds they represent as you share Today's News, as you talk with children about their writing, and as you reread the theme-related trade books.

DECODING AND PHONICS

LETTERS: *H, h*
SOUND/LETTER RELATIONSHIPS: /h/*H, h*

Developing Phonemic Awareness
Remind children of the different songs they have been learning for their concert. Here is another one they might enjoy.

Sing or play "Hambone," and encourage children to join in. Sing the song again and have children stand up when they hear the word *hambone*. Point out that *hambone* and *heard* begin with the same sound. Say these words again, accenting the beginning sound.

Hambone

Hambone, hambone, where you been?
Around the world and back again.

Hambone, hambone, what did you do?
I got a train and it fairly flew.

Hambone, hambone, have you heard?
Papa's gonna buy you a mockingbird.

♪ SING A SOUND AUDIOCASSETTES
Hambone

Developing Print Awareness

Write the first line of the song, "Hambone, hambone, where you been?" on the chalkboard or on chart paper. Encourage children to say the line with you and to follow as you point to each word.

Use the word mask to frame a capital and lowercase *h* in the first line.

- *Let's look at some* h*'s together. Here is a capital, or uppercase,* H *in the word* Hambone.

- *Here is a lowercase* h *in the word* hambone.

- *The letter* h *stands for the sound you hear at the beginning of the word* hambone. *Say* hambone *with me.*

Encourage children to come forward to point to and trace over with their fingers uppercase and lowercase *h*'s in the line.

You might want to create a bulletin board using construction paper to make a scene of singing and dancing animals and objects that include /h/ words. Encourage children to draw and label other pictures to add to the scene.

47

3 SING AND DANCE AWAY!

LITERATURE
Oh, A-Hunting We Will Go
by John Langstaff,
illustrated by
Nancy Winslow Parker

LISTENING LIBRARY
AUDIOCASSETTES
Oh, A-Hunting We Will Go

 SING & READ BOOKS AND
AUDIOCASSETTES
You'll Sing a Song
and I'll Sing a Song

EXPLORING PRINT
Big Book of Alphabet Rhymes and Chimes:
Hippity Hop to Bed

Alphabet Poster for Hh

ABC cards

Literature Activity Book: p. 44
Learning the Code: H, h

Practice Book: p. 14

BRWL: Letterbook H(12)

 A to EZ Handbook
• Predictable Books: p. 289
• Reading Recovery: p. 293

Performance Assessment Handbook

OTHER RESOURCES

• BIG BOOK STAND
• BIG BOOK POINTER
• CHART PAPER
• MARKERS
• POCKET CHART
• PICTURE CARDS
• LARGE SHEETS OF
  PAPER
• CRAYONS
• WORD MASK

Sharing Time

Today's News

As you write Today's News, point out the exclamation mark at the end of the sentence. Ask children to listen for the way your voice shows excitement.

As children gather around, invite them to begin singing the song "Oh, A-Hunting We Will Go."

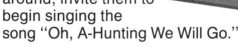

Let's go a-hunting today!

Creating Interest and Building Background

Because motivation matters!

Invite children to play a game as they sing "Oh, A-Hunting We Will Go."

- Children join hands and form a circle.

- One child, playing the fox, stands outside the circle.

- Children sing the song once and circle left as the fox skips and walks quickly to the right.

- As children sing the song again, the two children nearest the fox lift their arms and bring him into the circle.

- Children close the circle to trap the fox.

- On the words "let him go," children raise arms and let the fox go.

- The fox chooses a replacement, and the game begins again.

Children may enjoy continuing to play the game, pretending to be other animals.

READING AND WRITING

SHARING LITERATURE
Oh, A-Hunting We Will Go

BIG BOOK

REREAD THE STORY Invite individual children to name pictures of animals as you point to the words. Twelve children will be able to take part in this experience. If the group is enjoying it, begin the story again so twelve other children will have a chance.

PRINT AWARENESS

Musical Notes
- Show children the musical notes on page 32. Explain that music can be written down just as talk can be written down. Letters stand for the sounds in words. Musical notes stand for the sounds in music.

PHONEMIC AWARENESS

Initial Sounds: /h/h
- Ask children to go on a Word Hunt for words that begin with *H* or *h* (*him, house, hunting*). Encourage children to point to the words and to the letters.

Rhyming Words
- Pause for the word that rhymes with the animal's name and see if children can name it. Help children understand that every time the hunters catch an animal, they put it in something that rhymes with the animal's name.

And put him in a bunk,
And then we'll let him go!

24

Oh, a-hunting we will go,
A-hunting we will go;
We'll catch an armadillo

25

PATTERNED WRITING   Work with children to develop more rhymes to fit the text pattern. You may wish to make sentence strips to place in the pocket chart. Use picture cards for *fox* and *box*.

> Oh, a-hunting we will go,
> A-hunting we will go;
> We'll catch a fox
>   and put him in a box,
> And then we'll let him go!

Turn the pictures around so that *fox* and *box* are blank spaces. Start with animal names such as cat, dog, whale, goat, bear, deer, and snake to help children create new rhymes and pictures of animals and objects. Invite volunteers to place their pictures in the pocket chart.

> We'll catch a cat
>   and put him in a hat

RESPONDING TO LITERATURE

BOOK TALK   After sharing new observations about the story, invite children to think about other aspects of "Oh, A-Hunting We Will Go."

- *I started thinking about all the endangered animals in the world. I'm glad the author, John Langstaff, always let the animals go! I was relieved when I got to the last verse and realized that the story was a game of pretend. What did you think while you were reading the story?*

- *What animal was your favorite? Why did you like what happened to it?*

MAKING A CLASS BIG BOOK   Invite each child to draw a picture of a rhyme and write it on a large sheet of paper. Laminate the pages and make them into a class Big Book for everyone to read.

PERFORM THE SONG   Play the song on the LISTENING LIBRARY AUDIOCASSETTE as children march around the room. Or, choose instruments to use as the class performs the verses of the song together as they march around the school or onto the playground. Invite pairs to sing each verse.

EXPLORING PRINT LEARNING THE CODE

HANDS ON LANGUAGE

DECODING AND PHONICS

LETTERS: *H, h*
SOUND/LETTER RELATIONSHIPS: */h/H, h*

Developing Phonemic Awareness

Remind children that they are learning about the sounds of language and the letters that stand for those sounds. Ask children to listen as you read "Hippity Hop to Bed" on page 15 in the *Big Book of Alphabet Rhymes and Chimes*. As you come to words that begin with *h*, slightly emphasize the initial sound. Repeat the rhyme a few times, encouraging children to chime in.

• *Listen to the sound you hear at the beginning of* hippity *and* hop. *What other words do we know that begin with the same sound?*

Developing Print Awareness

Display "Hippity Hop to Bed" on page 15 of the *Big Book of Alphabet Rhymes and Chimes* and say the rhyme with children. Use the Big Book pointer or a word mask to point out or frame words that begin with an uppercase or lowercase *h*.

Hh

Hippity Hop to Bed

Hippity hop to bed,
I'd rather stay up instead.
But! When Daddy says "must,"
There's nothing else, just
Hippity, hoppity,
Hippity, hoppity,
Hippity, hoppity,
Hippity, hippity, hop!
To bed!

■ **Literature Activity Book:** page 44

Big Book of Alphabet Rhymes and Chimes,
page 15

52

Reread the rhyme and encourage children to act out the "hippity, hoppity" movements a frog would make as he hopped to bed.

Then display the Alphabet Poster and ABC cards for Hh, or write the letters on the chalkboard or on cards of your own.

Have children compare the *h*'s on the Big Book page with the letters on the poster and cards. Encourage children to talk about the horse pictured on the poster.

Remind children that the letter *h* stands for the sound /h/ in the words *hippity* and *hop*. Point out to children that many different words begin with /h/. Talk about any children's names that do.

Invite pairs of children to go on a Word Hunt around the room to find words on charts, signs, and in books that begin with the same sound and letter as *hippity* and *hop*. Have them copy the words on cards and then share and display them on the bulletin board.

TEAM WORK/THEME WORK
Take this opportunity to have children begin work on the welcome poster for the Song and Dance Concert. See pages 38–41.

INTO THE LEARNING CENTERS
Encourage children to visit the Hands On! Language Center to use the resources there for more activities with sounds and letters. See page 100.

4 SING AND DANCE AWAY!

LITERATURE
Max by Rachel Isadora

SONGS AND STORIES
AUDIOCASSETTES
STORY SONGS:
Movement Music—March from *The Nutcracker*

SING & READ BOOKS AND
AUDIOCASSETTES
You'll Sing a Song and I'll Sing a Song

EXPLORING PRINT
*Big Book of Alphabet Rhymes
and Chimes:* Hippity Hop to Bed

Rhyme and Chime Strips:
  Hippity Hop to Bed

Learning the Code: H, h

BRWL: Letterbook H(12)

 STAFF DEVELOPMENT A to EZ Handbook
  • Masking: p. 273
  • Pocket Chart: p. 285

Performance Assessment Handbook

MAX
story & pictures by
Rachel Isadora

OTHER RESOURCES

• BIG BOOK STAND
• BIG BOOK POINTER
• CHART PAPER
• MARKERS
• SCARVES
• CRAYONS
• POCKET CHART
• WORD MASK

LITERACY SUPPORT:
Building Language and Concepts

**For children acquiring English and/or
needing more intensive support, you
may wish to incorporate the following
suggestions into the basic lesson plan.**

Before reading the selection, show the class a segment of a
ballet film. Point out the graceful way in which ballet dancers
move to the music. Emphasize that ballet dancers are both
female and male. Afterwards, invite children to pretend to be
ballet dancers.

Before reading the selection, ask children to brainstorm what
they know about baseball and ballet.

SHARING TIME

TODAY'S NEWS

As you write and read Today's News, point to the word *dance* and remind children that one of the Theme Words is *dancer.* Talk about the question mark and what it means.

Do you play sports?
Do you like to dance?
You can do both!

CREATING INTEREST AND BUILDING BACKGROUND

Because motivation matters!

To prepare children for a book about baseball and ballet, first talk with children about the game of baseball.

- *Have you ever been to or played in a baseball game? What did you see or do?*

- *Do you have a brother or sister or friend who plays baseball? What do they do in the game?*

- *How do you move when you, your friends, or your brother or sister play baseball?*

- *How do you think baseball and dancing could be alike?*

Then play Movement Music on the STORY SONGS AUDIOCASSETTE and distribute scarves for children to use as they move or dance to the music. Suggest that they move as if they were playing baseball. Make this time a no-talking time, letting children hear and feel the music.

♪ SONGS AND STORIES AUDIOCASSETTES
STORY SONGS: Movement Music—March from *The Nutcracker*

READING AND WRITING

SHARING LITERATURE
Max

LOOK IT OVER   Hold up the cover of *Max,* read the name of the title, and point to it with your finger. Point to the author/illustrator's name, Rachel Isadora.

Talk with children about what they notice about the cover. From the illustration on the cover and on the title page, invite children to guess what the story will be about.

SHARE THE STORY   As you read, help children find Max in the illustrations.

About the Author/Illustrator

Share with children that Rachel Isadora is a writer who was a ballerina. She began dancing when she walked into her older sister's dance class when she was just a toddler.

Recently, Rachel Isadora has made several trips to South Africa with her news editor husband, James Turner. Her latest books take place in South Africa.

Share Rachel Isadora's dedication to her parents and Grandfather Max and ask children why they think the author called the book *Max.*

On Saturday mornings he walks with his sister Lisa to her dancing school. The school is on the way to the park.
8

One Saturday when they reach the school, Max still has lots of time before the game is to start. Lisa asks him if he wants to come inside for a while.
9

RESPONDING TO LITERATURE

BOOK TALK   Invite children to share their reactions to the book. Share your own experience playing baseball or taking dance lessons.

You may want to present some of the questions below to get more sharing started.

- *How do you think baseball players and ballet dancers are alike?*

- *Do you think Max will tell his friends on the baseball team about going to dance class?*

JOURNAL WRITING   Invite children to draw or write about the story in their journals. You may wish to write in your own journal about something memorable from the story as children write. After writing, ask children if they would like to share what they wrote with the group.

You may want to use the following prompts as ways to help them begin thinking about writing and drawing.

- *What could Lisa, Max's sister, learn from going to baseball practice with him?*

- *Write and draw about yourself playing baseball or taking ballet lessons.*

STORY THEATER   As you read the story, children will enjoy pantomiming the movements Max makes. Invite everyone in the class to play the role of Max.

TEAM WORK/THEME WORK
Ask children to decide whether they want to perform a scarf dance during the Song and Dance Concert. If so, set aside time for them to invent steps and movements and to practice them. See pages 38–41 and 94–95.

ITIS GD HTHI I love Book

**Caitlin is beginning to reread what she writes. The word *book* was added to this response when Caitlin reread and realized her message was incomplete.
Caitlin read her message like this: "It is good. He jumps high. I love that book."**

INTO THE LEARNING CENTERS
Today would be a good day to invite children into the Writing Center where they can make a Big Book of their favorite songs to dance to. See page 101.

EXPLORING PRINT

DEVELOPING CONCEPTS OF PRINT

Using the Rhyme and Chime Strips gives children a Hands On! Language experience that allows them to explore important concepts of print.

CONCEPTS OF PRINT
Directionality, Words

Hippity Hop to Bed

Hippity hop to bed,
I'd rather stay up instead.
But! When Daddy says "must,"
There's nothing else, just
Hippity, hoppity,
Hippity, hoppity,
Hippity, hoppity,
Hippity, hippity, hop!
To bed!

Hh

Big Book of Alphabet Rhymes and Chimes, page 15

Developing Print Awareness

Display page 15 in the *Big Book of Alphabet Rhymes and Chimes* and encourage children to recite "Hippity Hop to Bed" with you as you point to each word.

Use the strips and word cards from the Rhyme and Chime Strips shown below to build the rhyme in the pocket chart. Recite the rhyme as you build it.

Hippity hop to bed,			
I'd rather stay up instead.			
But! When Daddy says "must,"			
There's nothing else, just			
Hippity,	hoppity,		
Hippity,	hoppity,		
Hippity,	hoppity,		
Hippity,	hippity,	hop!	
To bed!			

Talk about words that are the same and point to them. Take the word cards for *Hippity* out of the pocket chart and ask five children to hold them. Have each child count the number of letters in each word after you model the process.

Display the word cards for *hoppity* and *hop*. Ask children what they notice about these two words. Which word has more letters? Which word is longer?

As you replace all word cards in the pocket chart, invite children to recite the rhyme with you again.

INTO THE LEARNING CENTERS
Ailow children to use the *Big Book of Alphabet Rhymes and Chimes,* the Rhyme and Chime Strips, and the word cards to build the rhyme "Hippity Hop to Bed" in the pocket chart in the Hands On! Language Center. See page 100.

5
SING AND DANCE AWAY!

LITERATURE
Max by Rachel Isadora

SING & READ BOOKS AND
AUDIOCASSETTES
You'll Sing a Song
and I'll Sing a Song

EXPLORING PRINT
Alphabet Poster for Hh

Rhyme and Chime Strips:
  Hippity Hop to Bed

Learning the Code: H, h

BRWL: Letterbook H(12)

A to EZ Handbook
  • Environmental Print: p. 255
  • Pointing: p. 287

Performance Assessment Handbook

OTHER RESOURCES

• BIG BOOK STAND
• BIG BOOK POINTER
• CHART PAPER
• MARKERS
• CRAYONS
• POCKET CHART
• WORD MASK

SHARING TIME

TODAY'S NEWS

As you write and read Today's News, remind children that Max is a dancer. Invite a volunteer to point to the word *Max*.

Let's dance along with Max again!

CREATING INTEREST AND BUILDING BACKGROUND

Because motivation matters!

To help children understand the idea in *Max* that boys and girls can learn from each other, introduce the poem "Don't Dress Your Cat in an Apron" by Dan Greenberg. You may wish to reread it with children chiming in on the rhyming words and repeating the last stanza as a group. Encourage children to talk about what the poet means by the last stanza.

You may wish to copy the poem onto chart paper and display it in the Reading or Writing Centers.

Don't Dress Your Cat in an Apron

Don't dress your cat in an apron
Just 'cause he's learning to bake.
Don't put your horse in a nightgown
Just 'cause he can't stay awake.
Don't dress your snake in a muu-muu
Just 'cause he's off on a cruise.
Don't dress your whale in galoshes
If she really prefers overshoes.

A person should wear what he wants to
And not just what other folks say.
A person should do what she likes to—
A person's a person that way.

—Dan Greenberg

READING AND WRITING

SHARING LITERATURE
Max

REREAD THE STORY   Invite children to follow Max through the story, paying special attention to how his feelings about ballet change. Have children listen for the ballet words and for the baseball words.

PRINT AWARENESS

Exclamation Marks
- Point out the exclamation marks on pages 26, 28, and 30. Ask children to say these phrases in a way that shows great excitement. *How would a radio announcer say "Strike One!" "Strike Two!" and "Home Run!"?*

Environmental Print
- Point out the print on signs in the illustrations, such as Home/Visitors, Runs/Strikes/Balls/Outs on page 7. Ask children to identify the signs on pages 8 and 22.

INTO THE LEARNING CENTERS
After talking about the pattern of Strike One and Strike Two, you may wish to direct children to the Math Center where they can further explore numerical patterns. See page 102.

RESPONDING TO LITERATURE

BOOK TALK   Share thoughts about the story that you might have wondered about since the first reading. Then invite children to focus on predicting.

- *When you make a prediction, you make a guess about what will happen next. Good readers make predictions as they read. They use information in the story to make a guess. When Max was batting, did you predict he would get a hit? Did you predict that he would hit a home run?*

- *What information did you use to make your prediction?*

Strike one!

26

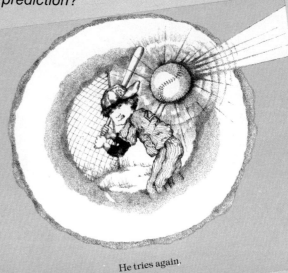

He tries again.

27

WRITING ABOUT BASEBALL OR BALLET   Work together to prepare a semantic map of words in the story that have to do with ballet and with baseball. Write the map on chart paper and read each of the words with children. Then invite children to write and draw about baseball or ballet, using words from the semantic map.

pas de chat

barre — ballet — leaps

split — warm up

team

bat

baseball — home run

strike

DRAMATIZE THE STORY   Take children outside if possible and invite them to be baseball players and ballet dancers. Volunteers will be needed to play Max, his sister Lisa, the other dancers and baseball players, as well as spectators for the baseball game.

Play a game of T-ball with the ball on a cone so that everyone who wants to play can get up to bat.

TEAM WORK/THEME WORK

If children are interested in learning some ballet steps or movements to incorporate into the Song and Dance Concert, invite a ballet teacher or older student who studies ballet to instruct them. Set aside time for children to practice the movements and to select music to which they can dance. See pages 38–41 and 94–95.

DECODING AND PHONICS

LETTERS: *H, h*
SOUND/LETTER RELATIONSHIPS: /h/ *H, h*

CONCEPTS OF PRINT
Directionality, Words, Letters

Developing Phonemic Awareness
Remind children that they have been learning about the sound you hear at the beginning of words like *hunting, house, home run, head, hippity,* and *hop* (words found in *Oh, A-Hunting We Will Go* and *Max* as well as "Hippity Hop to Bed"). Ask children to suggest other words that have the same beginning sound.

Developing Print Awareness
Display the Alphabet Poster for Hh and point to the word *horse*. Frame the letter *h* in the word. Remind children that the letter *h* stands for the sound you hear at the beginning of the word *horse*.

Use the word cards from the Rhyme and Chime Strips for "Hippity Hop to Bed" to build the rhyme as shown below.

Hippity	hop	to	bed,	
I'd	rather	stay	up	instead.
But!	When	Daddy	says	"must,"
There's	nothing	else,	just	
Hippity,	hoppity,			
Hippity,	hoppity,			
Hippity,	hoppity,			
Hippity,	hippity,	hop!		
To	bed!			

Encourage children to say the rhyme with you as you point to each word with the Big Book pointer. Have children clap each time they hear a word with the same beginning sound as *horse*.

Ask children to recite the rhyme and clap again. This time remove any word card for which the children did not clap.

Hippity	hop	
Hippity,	hoppity,	
Hippity,	hoppity,	
Hippity,	hoppity,	
Hippity,	hippity,	hop!

Frame the first letter in each word and have children name it as an *h*. Emphasize that the letter *h* stands for the sound heard at the beginning of the words *hippity* and *hop*. Use letter cards for *H* and *h* from the Rhyme and Chime Strips to match the letter cards to the words that begin with those letters.

Review all the charts and other print resources in the classroom to find words that begin with the same sound and letter as *hop*.

INTO THE LEARNING CENTERS
Using letter stamps, sponge letters, and magnetic letters in the Hands On! Language Center is a motivating way for children to experiment with print. See page 100.

6

SING AND DANCE AWAY!

LITERATURE

Read Aloud Anthology
"The Twelve Dancing
Princesses"
a German fairy tale
by the Brothers Grimm

SING & READ BOOKS AND
AUDIOCASSETTES
You'll Sing a Song
and I'll Sing a Song

SONGS AND STORIES
AUDIOCASSETTES
STORY SONGS:
Dancin' to the Beat

EXPLORING PRINT

SING A SOUND AUDIOCASSETTES
The Muffin Man

Learning the Code: M, m

Practice Book: p. 15

BRWL: Letterbook M(17)

A to EZ Handbook
• Dramatic Play: p. 250
• Dramatization: p. 252

Performance Assessment Handbook

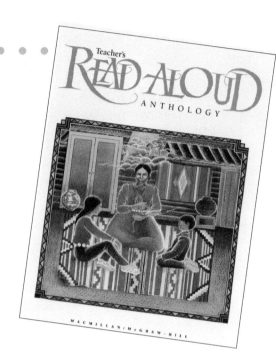

OTHER RESOURCES

• MURAL PAPER
• GLITTER, SEQUINS, FOIL
• PROPS SUCH AS
  CROWNS, CAPES,
  WAND, CLOAK,
  SOLDIER'S HAT
• WORD MASK

SHARING TIME

TODAY'S NEWS

Write and read Today's News, tracking each word as you read. Ask children to talk about where they think princesses might go to dance.

Where do princesses go to dance? Today we will find out.

CREATING INTEREST AND BUILDING BACKGROUND

Because motivation matters!

To prepare for "The Twelve Dancing Princesses," ask children to form pairs with one child being the dancer and the other one being the shadow. As you play the song "Dancin' to the Beat," encourage the shadow to follow the dancer's movements closely. When the music stops, partners should change roles and dance again. Remind children that one of the Theme Words is *dancer.*

Dancin' to the Beat

Chorus
Fast dance, slow dance, any-kind-you-know
   dance,
Hokey-pokey, hustle, jitterbug, bump;
Come on and groove it, all you gotta do is
   move it,
Get your arms, legs, body, feet—dancin' to the
   beat!

I've got rhythm, I've got soul,
But sometimes I feel out of control,
So I put on some music, get up on my feet,
Now I'm all together—dancin' to the beat!

Chorus

I dance at parties, I dance at home,
I dance when I'm talkin' on the telephone,
I dance in my bedroom, I dance in the street,
Oh, I'm so happy—dancin' to the beat!

I dance in the winter, I dance in the spring,
I dance no matter what the weather may bring,
I move fast when it's chilly, I move slow in the
   heat,
But it's always the season for dancin' to the
   beat!

Chorus

—Joanne Olshansky

 SONGS AND STORIES AUDIOCASSETTES
STORY SONGS: Dancin' to the Beat

READING AND WRITING

SHARING LITERATURE
"The Twelve Dancing Princesses"

SHARE THE STORY   As you tell or read the story, invite children to visualize, or see the pictures in their minds. Feel free to tell the story in your own way to make it understandable for children.

About the Story

Developing Multicultural Awareness

Share information with children that this folk tale comes from the Brothers Grimm. These two brothers, named Wilhelm and Jacob, tried to collect all the stories they could find in Germany. They collected the stories from storytellers and from books. Point out Germany on a world map or globe.

■ **Read Aloud Anthology:** pages 36–39

RESPONDING TO LITERATURE

BOOK TALK   Invite children to give personal comments about their reactions to the story. Encourage questions about the language or the characters in the folk tale.

You may want to use some of these questions to expand their understanding of "The Twelve Dancing Princesses."

- *Those princesses must have loved to dance! Would you have liked to have been with them?*

- *Did you predict that the soldier would choose the younger daughter as his wife? Were there other things in the story that turned out differently than you predicted?*

- *I wonder if the princesses will be able to go back to the underground castle. Do you think they will? Did you wonder about the "time of enchantment"?*

MAKE A STORY MURAL   Invite children to write and draw about the story on mural paper. Provide materials children could use to make the mural fairy-tale-like, such as glitter, sequins, and foil. Add these to the underground scenes of trees with silver and gold leaves, a lake with princesses and boats, and a brightly lighted castle.

STORY THEATER   As you retell the story, invite children to choose roles to play. A dramatization of the story will require these actors. You may want to use props such as crowns, capes, a wand, a cloak, and a soldier's hat.

12 princesses   the king
12 princes   the old woman
the soldier

TEAM WORK/THEME WORK
Take this opportunity to have children write their own proclamations announcing the Song and Dance Concert. This is also a good time to have them work in the Writing Center to prepare invitations for guests they wish to invite. See pages 38–41, 94–95, and 101.

INTO THE LEARNING CENTERS
Today would be a good day to direct children to the Dramatic Play Center where they can become dancers who will perform in front of an audience. See page 99.

EXPLORING PRINT LEARNING THE CODE

In the Exploring Print lessons for this theme, children will learn about H, h *and* M, m *and the sounds they represent. Take advantage of opportunities to point out these letters and the sounds they represent as you share Today's News, as you talk with children about their writing, and as you read the theme-related trade books.*

DECODING AND PHONICS

LETTERS: *M, m*
SOUND/LETTER RELATIONSHIPS: /m/*M, m*

Developing Phonemic Awareness
Remind children that Max and the twelve princesses all danced to beautiful music. Here is some more music that they might enjoy. Sing or play "The Muffin Man" and encourage children to join in.

> **The Muffin Man**
>
> Oh, do you know the muffin man,
> The muffin man, the muffin man?
> Oh, do you know the muffin man
> Who lives on Drury Lane?

♪ SING A SOUND AUDIOCASSETTES
The Muffin Man

Play a name response version of the song by asking children to sit in a circle. Place their name cards in a pile, facedown. Pick up a name card and display it as you and the children sing the first part of the song. The child whose name card is displayed responds by singing the second part of the song.

> Oh yes, I know the muffin man,
> The muffin man, the muffin man.
> Oh yes, I know the muffin man
> Who lives on Drury Lane.

Ask children to name the words in the song that begin with the same sound as the word *music*.

Developing Print Awareness
Write the song title and first line of "The Muffin Man" on the chalkboard or on chart paper. Encourage children to say the title and first line with you and to follow as you point to each word.

> The Muffin Man
>
> Oh, do you know the muffin man,

Use the word mask to frame capital and lowercase *m*'s in the words *Muffin* and *muffin*.

- Let's look at some m's together. Here is a capital, or uppercase, M in the word Muffin. What other word can you find in the title that begins with capital M?

- Here is a lowercase m in the word man. What other word can you find in this line that has a lowercase m in it?

- The letter m stands for the sound you hear at the beginning of the words music, muffin, *and* man. Say music *with me.*

Encourage children to come forward to point to and trace over with their fingers the uppercase and lowercase *m*'s in the title and first line.

You might want to put the *m*'s on a Word Wall like the one below.

Encourage children to add "musical" words to the Word Wall.

7

SING AND DANCE AWAY!

LITERATURE
The Little Band by James Sage,
   illustrated by Keiko Narahashi

SING & READ BOOKS AND
AUDIOCASSETTES
You'll Sing a Song
and I'll Sing a Song

EXPLORING PRINT
*Big Book of Alphabet Rhymes
and Chimes:* Miss Mary Mack

Alphabet Poster for Mm

ABC cards

Literature Activity Book: p. 45
   Learning the Code: M, m

Practice Book: p. 16

BRWL: Letterbook M(17)

 A to EZ Handbook
   • Finger Plays: p. 256
   • Invented Spelling: p. 260

Performance Assessment Handbook

OTHER RESOURCES

• MURAL PAPER
• MARKERS, PAINT OR
   CRAYONS
• BIG BOOK STAND
• BIG BOOK POINTER

LITERACY SUPPORT:
Building Language and Concepts

**For children acquiring English and/or
needing more intensive support, you
may wish to incorporate the following
suggestions into the basic lesson plan.**

While reading, explain the remarks by the townspeople about
the little band. For example, words and phrases such as:
pleased, charming, and *what a wonder* may need to be clarified
for children. Encourage children to think of other words that
could have been used.

After reading the selection, invite six volunteers to act out being
part of "the little band."

SHARING TIME

TODAY'S NEWS

As you write and read Today's News, invite children to guess what or who the Little Band is.

The little band is coming to town! Will they sing? Will they dance?

CREATING INTEREST AND BUILDING BACKGROUND

Because motivation matters!

Talk together about the instruments you and the children know about. Encourage them to describe the way each instrument is played.

Introduce the finger play "The Finger Band," which is sung to the tune of "The Mulberry Bush." As they sing, invite children to pantomime playing each instrument and conclude by singing the final verse and hiding their fingers behind their backs.

The Finger Band

The Finger Band has come to town,
Come to town, come to town.
The Finger Band has come to town,
So early in the morning.

The Finger Band can play the drums,
Play the drums, play the drums.
The Finger Band can play the drums,
So early in the morning.

The Finger Band can play the piano,
         . . . flute,
         . . . harp,
         . . . tambourine, etc.

The Finger Band has gone away,
Gone away, gone away.
The Finger Band has gone away,
So early in the morning.

READING AND WRITING

SHARING LITERATURE
The Little Band

LOOK IT OVER   Read the title of the book and name of the author and illustrator.

Open the book to display both front and back covers simultaneously so children can find out more about "The Little Band." Invite children to identify each of the instruments the little band members are playing.

SHARE THE STORY   As you read, ask children to describe what is happening in the illustrations.

About the Author and Illustrator

Share the information that James Sage is an American writer who now lives in England. He used to work with educational films in the United States.

Keiko Narahashi has illustrated a number of children's books in the last few years. She is originally from Japan and now lives in New York City. She has been playing the piano since she was four years old and studied to be a classical pianist at one time. Because she didn't like to perform, she turned to drawing and painting.

"Charming! Charming!" murmured the old folks as they rocked to the rhythm of the drum.

18

"What a wonder!" exclaimed the sea captain, who thought he had seen everything.

19

RESPONDING TO LITERATURE

BOOK TALK   Invite children to share their personal reactions to the book. You may want to present some of the prompts below to get the discussion started, or you may want to talk about your own experiences with parades or bands.

- *Have you ever heard a band marching through a town or a mall or our school? Describe how it made you feel.*

- *Did any of the people and places remind you of people and places that you know?*

- *What was your favorite part of the story? I liked when the author said "The music made the dogs bark and the cats howl and the chickens cluck and the sheep baa with contentment."*

- *Can you imagine what "The Little Band" might sound like? Hum how they would sound for us.*

JOURNAL WRITING   Invite children to write about their favorite scenes. As children write, model writing in your own journal.

MAKING A STORY MURAL   Invite children to draw backdrops or story murals to accompany their retellings of the story. Provide mural paper, markers, paint, or crayons to show the road and the route of "The Little Band." Help children sequence the story events.

As you reread the story, children can position themselves alongside the story mural and retell the story when you come to their parts.

I wor weɑl
Dᵉ cmᵓ fwehm

It's apparent through Margaret's journal entry that *The Little Band* really left her wondering. Such a journal entry could serve as a wonderful discussion opener. Margaret read her message like this: "I wonder where they are coming from."

INTO THE LEARNING CENTERS
You may wish to have children visit the Art Center today so that their fingers can dance and paint to the sound of music. See page 104.

HANDS ON LANGUAGE

Exploring Print — LEARNING THE CODE

DECODING AND PHONICS

LETTERS: *M, m*
SOUND/LETTER RELATIONSHIPS: /m/M, m

Developing Phonemic Awareness
Ask children to listen as you read "Miss Mary Mack" on page 20 in the *Big Book of Rhymes and Chimes.* As you come to words that begin with *m,* slightly emphasize the initial sound.

- *Listen to the sound you hear at the beginning of Miss, Mary, and Mack. What other words do we know that begin with the same sound?*

Repeat the rhyme a few times, encouraging children to chime in.

Developing Print Awareness
Display "Miss Mary Mack" on page 20 of the *Big Book of Alphabet Rhymes and Chimes* and say the rhyme with children. Use the Big Book pointer to point out words that begin with *M.*

Mm

Miss Mary Mack

Miss Mary Mack,
Mack, Mack,
All dressed in black,
black, black,
With silver buttons,
buttons, buttons,
All down her back,
back, back.

Big Book of Alphabet Rhymes and Chimes,
page 20

Mm
monkey

Then display the Alphabet Poster and ABC cards for Mm, or write the letters on the chalkboard and on cards of your own.

Have children compare the *M*'s on the Big Book page with the letters on the poster and card. Encourage children to talk about the monkey pictured on the poster.

■ **Literature Activity Book:** page 45

8
SING AND DANCE AWAY!

Sharing Time

TODAY'S NEWS

As you write and read Today's News, talk about how children could be part of a band that performed.

Let's join the little band and form a parade!

CREATING INTEREST AND BUILDING BACKGROUND

Because motivation matters!

Introduce a parade as a march in honor of a person or an event. Talk about parades children have been in or have seen. Introduce the parade song "Parade Came Marching" to children. Practice marching around the room as you and the children sing to the STORY SONGS AUDIOCASSETTE.

Parade Came Marching

The parade came marching through
   the town
Left right
The parade came marching through
   the town
Left right
Oh, we all came marching
with my Mom and Daddy watching
And we kept on marching through
   the town
Left right

—John Forster

SONGS AND STORIES AUDIOCASSETTES
STORY SONGS: Parade Came Marching

79

READING AND WRITING

SHARING LITERATURE
The Little Band

REREAD THE STORY   Invite children to locate the instruments in each illustration. As each of the townspeople is introduced, invite a child to point to that person.

PRINT AWARENESS

Environmental Print
Point out the signs the little band encounters on their march. Turn to page 11 and point to the POST OFFICE signs on the building. Ask children to look through the book to find additional examples. (See pages 12, 18, and 19.)

PHONEMIC AWARENESS

Initial Sounds: /m/m
Invite children to listen for words that have the same beginning sound as *music* as you read pages 10 and 13. (*marched, mailman, market, missing, marched*)

"Wait!" called the mayor,
who wanted to give a speech of welcome.
But the little band did not wait.
They marched past the town officials,
past the workmen enjoying a rest,
past the bride and groom leaving church,
past the smiling faces in the playground.

14   15

RESPONDING TO LITERATURE

BOOK TALK   Ask children if they have any thoughts to share since you last talked about the story. Share any new observations you may have, or use the following questions as prompts.

- *I noticed the band members' wild hats this time! Did you?*

- *Have you been thinking about the author's unanswered questions about the little band—who they were, why they had come, and where they were going? What do you think the answers are?*

- *Why does the author say "nothing was ever the same again?" What do you think has changed?*

- *What would you tell a friend about this story?*

WRITE NEWSPAPER ARTICLES   Divide children into three groups to write newspaper articles about the three unanswered questions. One group can write about who the little band was, another group can write about why they had come, and a third group can write about where they were going. Give children time to agree among themselves and then give them paper, pencils, and crayons to write the articles that answer their questions. Label their articles and place them on a wall or bulletin board.

WHO?	WHY?	WHERE?

STORY THEATER   Perform the story with you in the role of a wandering storyteller who narrates the action, and children as the little band and the townspeople. The little band will enjoy using instruments they have made as they wander through the school or outside on the school grounds.

TEAM WORK/THEME WORK
Take this opportunity to invite children to work on their costumes for the Song and Dance Concert. You may wish to suggest that they wear hats like those worn by the little band. See pages 38–41 and 94–95.

INTO THE LEARNING CENTERS
Today would be a good day to have children visit the Music Center where they can make pan pipes. See page 103. It would also be a good day to direct children to the Dramatic Play Center where they can use these instruments and act out the roles of the little band. See page 99.

EXPLORING PRINT   DEVELOPING CONCEPTS OF PRINT

Using the Rhyme and Chime Strips gives children a Hands On! Language experience that allows them to explore important concepts of print.

CONCEPTS OF PRINT
Directionality, Words

Miss Mary Mack

Miss Mary Mack,
Mack, Mack,
All dressed in black,
black, black,
With silver buttons,
buttons, buttons,
All down her back,
back, back.

Big Book of Alphabet Rhymes and Chimes, page 20

Developing Print Awareness

Display page 20 of the *Big Book of Alphabet Rhymes and Chimes* and encourage children to recite the rhyme with you as you point to each word.

Explain that there are many different words in the rhyme. Each word has a space in front of it and at the end of it.

Use the word cards cut from the Rhyme and Chime Strips for "Miss Mary Mack" to build the rhyme in the pocket chart as shown. Recite the rhyme as you build it in the pocket chart and encourage children to recite it with you, being careful not to get ahead of you.

Miss	Mary	Mack,		
Mack,	Mack,			
All	dressed	in	black,	
black,	black,			
With	silver	buttons,		
buttons,	buttons,			
All	down	her	back,	
back,	back.			

Use the picture cards to have children match the pictures of Mary Mack, her black dress, her silver buttons, and her back as you and the children recite the appropriate phrase.

Encourage children to pick out word cards that are the same:

Mack, Mack, Mack
black, black, black
back, back, back

What do they notice about the words?

INTO THE LEARNING CENTERS

Allow children to use the *Big Book of Alphabet Rhymes and Chimes*, the Rhyme and Chime Strips, and the word and picture cards to build the rhyme "Miss Mary Mack" in the pocket chart in the Hands On! Language Center. See page 100.

9

SING AND DANCE AWAY!

LITERATURE

Read Aloud Anthology
"The Clever Turtle"
a Hispanic folk tale
retold by Margaret H. Lippert

 SONGS AND STORIES
AUDIOCASSETTES
STORY SONGS:
Sambalele

SONGS AND STORIES
AUDIOCASSETTES
STORYTELLINGS:
The Clever Turtle

 SING & READ BOOKS AND
AUDIOCASSETTES
You'll Sing a Song
and I'll Sing a Song

Literature Activity Book: pp. 47–48
Tell a Tale

EXPLORING PRINT

Rhyme and Chime Strips:
Miss Mary Mack

Alphabet Poster for Mm

Learning the Code: M, m

BRWL: Letterbook M(17)

STAFF DEVELOPMENT A to EZ Handbook
- Phonemic Awareness: p. 281
- Retelling: p. 295

Performance Assessment Handbook

OTHER RESOURCES

- SMALL STONES
- MARKERS
- PIPE CLEANERS
- TOOTHPICKS
- SHOE BOXES
- TWIGS AND SAND
- CONSTRUCTION PAPER

SHARING TIME

TODAY'S NEWS

After you write Today's News, point out the word *clever*. Ask children to talk about what the word means. Then share with them that they will listen to a story from Brazil about a clever turtle who can play a flute and dance.

What's very smart, yet very slow? A clever turtle!

CREATING INTEREST AND BUILDING BACKGROUND

Because motivation matters!

Children can form a Brazilian conga line by putting their hands on the waist of the person in front of them and snaking around the room. Point out that this dance comes from the same country as "The Clever Turtle." As they dance to "Sambalele," children can make up their own steps or they may enjoy the challenge of trying these steps:

Step left, right, left, kick right foot.
Step right, left, right, kick left foot.

Sambalele

Sambalele missed the party.
Said he was not feeling hearty.
But when our feet started tapping,
He'd had enough of his napping.

Chorus
Samba, samba, samba, o-le!
Step here behind me and do as I say.
Samba, samba, samba this way.
Soon you'll be wanting to dance it all day.

Sambalele, come and sing it.
Soon you'll be ready to swing it.
Just clap your hands to the music,
Then you'll be ready to dance it.

*R*EADING AND WRITING

SHARING LITERATURE
"The Clever Turtle"

SHARE THE STORY   Invite children to listen for the sound of the turtle's flute as they listen to the STORYTELLINGS AUDIOCASSETTE or to you telling the story. Encourage them to chime in whenever they hear the "wheet-weedle-whoo" and "wheet-wheet-wheet-whoo" of the flute.

♪ SONGS AND STORIES AUDIOCASSETTES
STORYTELLINGS: The Clever Turtle

■ **Read Aloud Anthology:** pages 40–41

Developing Multicultural Awareness

About the Story

Share with children that the story is from the country of Brazil and is more than one hundred years old. Point out Brazil and the Amazon River on a map or globe. Children might be interested to learn that its length of 4,000 miles (6,437 km) makes the Amazon River the second longest in the world and that it carries more water than any other river on earth.

RESPONDING TO LITERATURE

BOOK TALK   Invite children to share any personal reactions to the story. You may want to use some of these questions to get the discussion started.

- *How did the turtle show that she was clever?*

- *Do you think the father ever found the clever turtle again? Why do you think so?*

- *Do you think the children were happy or sad that they didn't eat the clever turtle? If you had been one of the children, how would you have felt?*

JOURNAL WRITING   Invite children to react to the story by writing or drawing what they thought of the clever turtle. Encourage volunteers to share their responses with the group.

DIORAMA PERFORMANCES   Provide children with small stones. Have children paint their stones or color them with markers so that they look like turtle shells, and then add pipe cleaners to form a head, a tail, and feet. One front leg could be wrapped around a toothpick "flute." Have small groups of children construct forest and yard settings for the story in shoe boxes, using collected twigs, sand, or green and brown construction or tissue paper. Children may choose to add details such as a paper hut, a small box to serve as the turtle's cage, and small characters made out of pipe cleaners. Give each child a chance to retell the story to his or her group, using his or her turtle and the group's diorama. Encourage other group members to participate in the retelling by making flutelike music with their voices or with the instruments they make in the Music Center. See page 103.

DECODING AND PHONICS

LETTERS: *M, m*
SOUND/LETTER RELATIONSHIPS: /m/*M, m*

CONCEPTS OF PRINT
Directionality, Words, Letters

Developing Phonemic Awareness
Remind children that they have been learning about the sound you hear at the beginning of words like *Max, must, music, marched, market, mayor, man, meat, Miss,* and *Mary* (words from *Max, The Little Band,* and "The Clever Turtle," as well as "Miss Mary Mack"). Ask children to suggest other words that have the same beginning sound.

Developing Print Awareness
Display the Alphabet Poster for Mm and point to the word *monkey*. Frame the letter *m* in the word. Remind children that the letter *m* stands for the sound heard at the beginning of the word *monkey*.

Use the word cards from the Rhyme and Chime Strips for "Miss Mary Mack" to build the rhyme as shown.

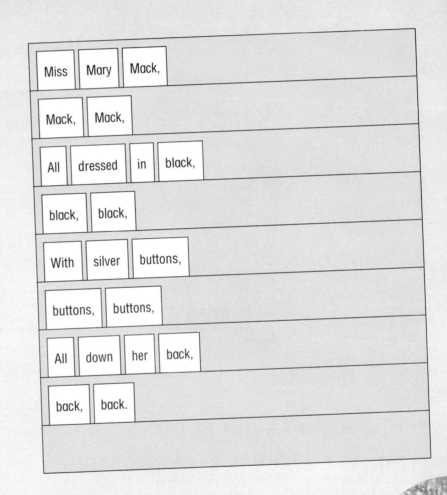

Miss	Mary	Mack,	
Mack,	Mack,		
All	dressed	in	black,
black,	black,		
With	silver	buttons,	
buttons,	buttons,		
All	down	her	back,
back,	back.		

Have children use the letter cards for *M* and *m* from the Rhyme and Chime Strips to match the letters to the words that begin with the letters.

Ask volunteers to come up and take a word card that begins with the sound /m/ and the letter *m*.

Review all the charts and other print resources in the classroom to find words that begin with the same sound and letter as *Miss*.

TEAM WORK/THEME WORK
Make time for children to finish preparations for the Song and Dance Concert. Encourage them to continue practicing any songs or dances that they do not yet feel comfortable performing. See pages 38–41 and 94–95.

INTO THE LEARNING CENTERS
Using letter stamps, sponge letters, and magnetic letters in the Hands On! Language Center is a motivating way for children to experiment with print. See page 100.

10 SING AND DANCE AWAY!

LITERATURE
Big Book of Songs:
You'll Sing a Song
and I'll Sing a Song

Big Book of Poems:
Singing-Time

 SING & READ BOOKS AND
AUDIOCASSETTES
You'll Sing a Song
and I'll Sing a Song

 SONGS AND STORIES
AUDIOCASSETTES
STORY SONGS:
You'll Sing a Song
and I'll Sing a Song

Oh, A Hunting We Will Go
    by John Langstaff,
    illustrated by
    Nancy Winslow Parker

Max by Rachel Isadora

The Little Band by James Sage,
    illustrated by Keiko Narahashi

Literature Activity Books: p. 49
    Responding to Literature

 A to EZ Handbook

   • Observation: p. 279

   • Risk-Free Environment: p. 297

Performance Assessment Handbook

OTHER RESOURCES

• BIG BOOK STAND
• BIG BOOK POINTER

Sharing Time

TODAY'S NEWS

Write and read Today's News, pointing to each word as you read. Remind children that the Theme Words are *singer* and *dancer,* and ask them how singing and dancing makes them feel.

Singers! Dancers! Music! Today is our Song and Dance Concert.

WRAPPING IT UP

To establish a celebratory mood, reread the Theme Poem "Singing-Time" on pages 18–19 in the *Big Book of Poems.* Then have children join in as you sing or play the Theme Song, "You Sing a Song and I'll Sing a Song."

Display the song on pages 16–17 in the *Big Book of Songs.* Point to the words with the Big Book pointer as children sing along.

♪ SONGS AND STORIES AUDIOCASSETTES
STORY SONGS: You'll Sing a Song and I'll Sing a Song

You'll Sing a Song and I'll Sing a Song

You'll sing a song,
And I'll sing a song,
And we'll sing a song together.

You'll sing a song,
And I'll sing a song,
In warm or wintry weather.
In warm or wintry weather.

Ella Jenkins

Big Book of Songs, pages 16–17

Reading and Writing

SHARING LITERATURE

LOOK IT OVER   Display the books *Oh, A-Hunting We Will Go; Max;* and *The Little Band.* Invite children to select one book to reread.

REREAD THE STORY   Reread the chosen selection. If children choose *Oh, A-Hunting We Will Go,* assign partners to sing aloud each verse after you read it aloud. If children choose *Max* or *The Little Band,* call on volunteers to act out different story events as you read.

Review the letters children have learned about by asking children to find and listen for words that begin with *h* and *m.* For additional practice, you may wish to use the Phonics Activity Sheets on pages 109–110.

RESPONDING TO LITERATURE

BOOK TALK   Encourage children to talk about the books in the theme and how they are alike and different. You may want to present some of the questions below to get the discussion started.

- *How is music or dancing important in each book?*

- *If you could go "hunting," go to Max's dance class, or march with the Little Band, which would you want to do? Why?*

- *Which book did you like best? Why?*

- *Which books had events that could really happen? How do you know?*

- *Did anyone in the books remind you of anyone you know? Who was it?*

JOURNAL WRITING   Invite children to draw or write in their journals about the book or books they liked best. Encourage volunteers to share their journals with the group.

A Song and Dance Concert

Let the singing and dancing begin as children perform their concert for invited guests! After the concert, invite the guests to join in the dancing and singing, too!

COME TO OUR SONG AND DANCE CONCERT!

Introduction

The Hokey-Pokey
Oh, A-Hunting We Will Go
Eency, Weency Spider
Old Brass Wagon
Tinga Layo

Into the Learning Centers!

▼

Learning Centers can be places where children learn independently, from one another, and from you! Engaging activities can motivate children to become literacy explorers!

A to EZ Handbook
• Learning Centers: p. 270

READING CENTER
—*Singing and Dancing with Books! page 98*

DRAMATIC PLAY CENTER
—*Show Time! page 99*

HANDS ON! LANGUAGE CENTER
—*Exploring Language through Manipulatives! page 100*

WRITING CENTER
—*Making a Big Book of Our Favorite Songs! page 101*

MATH CENTER
—*Clapping Patterns/ Counting Notes/Making Music! page 102*

MUSIC CENTER
—*Making Pan Pipes! page 103*

ART CENTER
—*Finger Dancing! page 104*

GAMES CENTER
—*Games for Singing and Dancing Away! page 105*

Reading Center

SINGING AND DANCING WITH BOOKS!

Resources ***The Little Band* *Max* *Big Book of Oh, A-Hunting We Will Go* * *Big Book of Songs* * *Big Book of Poems* * *Sing & Read Little Books* * *Listening Library Audiocassettes* * *Songs and Stories Audiocassettes* *** theme-related books

Setting Up! Display books for shared and emergent readings. Put up signs to encourage children to share the books in the Reading Center! Display headlines from newspapers about dance, sports, and other activities that involve movement. Display the words to songs that children have learned in *Sing and Dance Away!*

- Place the Sing & Read Little Book and Audiocassette for "You'll Sing a Song and I'll Sing a Song" by the tape recorder.

- Have the Listening Library Audiocassette for *Oh, A-Hunting We Will Go* available.

- Invite children to listen to "You'll Sing a Song and I'll Sing a Song" and "The Clever Turtle" on the SONGS AND STORIES AUDIOCASSETTES.

Reading away!

Centers in Action! Encourage children to explore the books and materials displayed. Continue to add books, songs, and materials to the center, and invite children to do the same. Display the theme Big Books—and keep the Big Book pointer within easy reach so that children can model being teachers!

Children will enjoy singing "Oh, A-Hunting We Will Go" and other songs from the theme as they "conduct" the song using the Big Book pointer.

Dramatic Play Center

Show Time!

Resources large piece of butcher paper * construction paper * crayons or markers * rope * sheet * scissors * song and music sheets * chairs * a large, flat box * strip of cardboard or oaktag * strip of white paper * black marker * tape * polystyrene ball * cardboard paper towel tube * shoe box * rubber bands

Setting Up!

- Hang the butcher paper as a backdrop.

- Glue a strip of white paper to the strip of cardboard or oaktag and draw piano keys on it. Glue or tape the strip of piano keys to the bottom edge of the flat box to make a piano. Place the song and music sheets on the piano.

- A child can paint or color the polystyrene ball gray and stick the paper towel tube into it to make a microphone.

- If possible, attach the rope so that it stretches parallel to the backdrop and hang the sheet over the rope to form a curtain. Then arrange the chairs in front of the curtain for the audience.

- Make the Big Book pointer or a wand available for children to use as a baton when they are playing the role of conductor.

Centers in Action! Encourage children to become singers, dancers, conductors, announcers, and musicians by performing in front of the backdrop for an audience.

- Children can make masks, mustaches, eyeglasses, and other props out of construction paper.

And the show goes on!

- Children can wrap three rubber bands around an open box such as a shoe box and then pluck the rubber band strings to make a musical instrument.

- Children may also decorate the backdrop to suit their performances.

- You may wish to take this opportunity to have children write invitations to their performances.

HANDS ON! LANGUAGE CENTER

EXPLORING LANGUAGE THROUGH MANIPULATIVES

Resources *pocket chart and stand* * *ABC cards* * *slate board and chalk* * *sponge letters* * *letter stamps* * *linked letter cubes* * paper * pads * pencils * crayons * letter blocks * *magnetic letters* * stencils

Setting Up! Children may explore language independently, but you may also wish to suggest the theme-related activities described under Centers in Action!

Centers in Action!

• Children can use sponge letters, letter stamps, and stencils to print and trace the letters in their names as well as the names of the people they like to sing and dance with.

• Children can work together to use sponge letters and letter stamps to print and trace letters and words from *The Little Band, Max,* and *Oh, A-Hunting We Will Go.*

• Children may also enjoy using sponge letters, letter stamps, and stencils to print and trace the letters in their favorite songs.

• Children can draw pictures of themselves singing and dancing and then label the pictures.

Writing Center

MAKING A BIG BOOK OF OUR FAVORITE SONGS

Resources large sheets of butcher paper * crayons * markers * pencils * scissors

Setting Up! Cut butcher paper into approximately 34″ x 22″ sheets.

Centers in Action! Encourage children to make a Big Book of their favorite songs. Children can draw and write on the sheets of butcher paper. Put pages together in a Big Book called *Our Favorite Songs.* Children may wish to display the Big Book in the Dramatic Play Center.

Provide time for children to write the invitations and posters announcing the Team Work/Theme Work Song and Dance Concert.

Writing about our favorite songs and dances!

Math Center

CLAPPING PATTERNS

Resources plastic container * four glasses of the same size * measuring cup * stick or spoon * index cards * markers *

Setting Up! Display a plastic container of water, four glasses, a measuring cup, and a stick. Draw different numbers of quarter notes on index cards, one amount per card. On the back of each card, write the numeral for the number of notes on that card.

Get children started in the Math Center by clapping a pattern such as *clap, pause, clap, pause.* Ask children to repeat the pattern.

Centers in Action! Invite children to take part in one of the following activities.

- **Continue the Pattern:** Invite children to introduce their own clapping patterns such as the one you already introduced. Encourage other children to join in the clapping and watch the followers of the clapping patterns become the leaders of the group!

Count the Notes!

- Children can count the notes on each card, then turn them over to check their answers.

- Children can also work with partners, one child counting the number of notes as the other child checks the answer.

- Children can use counters or buttons to count out the same number as the number of notes on each card.

- **Musical Glasses:** Invite children to measure amounts of water and to fill each of the glasses with a different amount. Children may then use the stick or spoon to tap each glass to obtain a different tone. Children may enjoy numbering the glasses, one to four, and then tapping out a song such as *1,1, 2,2, 3,3, 4.*

Counting away!

Music Center

MAKING PAN PIPES!

Resources plastic straws or plastic piping * scissors * tape * clay

Setting Up! Cut straws into pieces of two, three, four, and five inches. Seal one end of each of these straws with a piece of clay or tape.

Centers in Action! With a little help, children can make pan pipes like the one played by the girl with the green leaf hat in *The Little Band.* These instruments are thousands of years old.

- Invite each child to choose 6 pieces of hollow plastic piping or straw pieces ranging in length from 2 to 8 inches.

- Seal one end of each tube with a piece of modeling clay or tape.

- Children can arrange the piping or straw pieces in order from shortest to longest.

- Tape the straws or piping together so that the open ends are level with each other.

Children will enjoy playing their pan pipes by placing the edge of the open end against their lower lips and blowing gently. As they explore playing their pan pipes, encourage children to discover how the length of the pipe affects the pitch of the notes. (Longer pipes give lower notes and shorter pipes give higher notes.)

Encourage children to be singers and dancers by singing and dancing to the songs that they know as they play their pan pipes. Children may like to dance as they move in a line, as in *The Little Band,* dance by themselves, as in *Max,* or dance together.

Making beautiful music to dance to!

Art Center

FINGER DANCING

Resources   paper * liquid starch * tempera powder * plastic containers for paint * paintbrushes * crayons * stones * paper towels * tape recorder * *Songs and Stories Audiocassettes*

Setting Up!   Arrange the materials on a table in the Art Center. Mix the liquid starch with the tempera powder to make paint. Set up the tape recorder to play the songs from the theme while children paint. Include some of your own favorites—jazz, folk songs, reggae, marches, or lullabies.

Centers in Action!   As children listen to the songs of the theme, they can create their own artwork or try one of the following activities:

- Children will enjoy finger painting freely, letting their fingers "dance" to the music they hear. Tell them to "let your fingers and hands move just the way the music tells you."

- Children may wish to draw with crayons on paper, then finger paint over the crayon drawings.

- Children may also enjoy drawing or painting pictures of dancing and singing from the stories they have read and heard.

- To make their own clever turtles, children can paint or draw on stones to make them look like turtles.

Remind children to sign their art and to provide labels or captions as well.

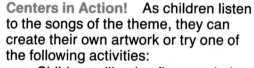

Creating art to the sound of music!

104

Games Center

GAMES FOR SINGING AND DANCING AWAY!

Resources   tape recorder * ***Songs and Stories Audiocassettes*** * balloons * rice

Setting Up!   Place some rice into a balloon (one for each child) and tie the balloon's end to make a "beanbag." Rewind the tape and prepare to play it.

Centers in Action!   Children may enjoy playing one or more of the following games.

- Invite children to play Oh, A-Hunting We Will Go by joining hands to form a circle. One child becomes the fox and stands outside of the circle. Then children sing "Oh, A-Hunting We Will Go" as they move left and the fox skips to the right. As children begin to sing the song again, the two children nearest to the fox bring him into the circle by lifting their arms up and then down on the other side of him. The children in the circle begin closing the circle to trap the fox, but as they sing "let him go," they should raise their arms and let the fox go. The fox then chooses a new fox and the game begins again.

- To play musical beanbags, children move around the room and place the beanbags on different parts of their bodies, such as their heads, knees, and shoulders, without letting the beanbags fall. When the song is over and the music stops, the children should freeze until the next song begins.

- Invite children to play a game of "Max Says" instead of "Simon Says." To play, children should stand in front of a volunteer who is "Max" and do what he or she does. "Max" may wish to perform some of the movements from the story *Max* for children to copy.

ACKNOWLEDGMENTS

Every effort has been made to trace the ownership of all copyrighted material and to secure the necessary permissions to reprint these selections. In the event of any question arising as to the use of any material, the editor and publisher, while expressing regret for any inadvertent error, will be happy to make the necessary correction in future printings.

The publisher gratefully acknowledges permission to reprint the following copyrighted material:

"Dancin' to the Beat," words and music by Joanne Olshansky. © 1987 JHO Music. Song can be heard on PIZZA BOOGIE, available as cassette, LP, or songbook from JHO Music, 11 Marshall Terrace, Wayland, MA 01778.

"Don't Dress Your Cat in an Apron" by Dan Greenberg, from FREE TO BE . . . YOU AND ME by Marlo Thomas and Associates. Copyright © 1974 Free to be Foundation, Inc. Used by Permission of Bantam Books, a division of Bantam Doubleday Dell Publishing Group, Inc.

"Mi Cuerpo Hace Musica," traditional Hispanic song translated and arranged © 1988 Sarah Pirtle. Appears on the recording THE WIND IS TELLING SECRETS, A Gentle Wind, Box 3103, Albany, NY 12203.

"Parade Came Marching," words and music by John Forster. © 1988 Limousine Music Company.

"Singing-Time" from THE FAIRY GREEN by Rose Fyleman. Copyright © 1923 by George H. Doran, Company. Reprinted by permission of Doubleday, a division of Bantam Doubleday Dell Publishing Group, Inc.

"You'll Sing a Song and I'll Sing a Song," © 1966 words and music by Ella Jenkins, Ell-Bern Publishing Company, 1844 North Mohawk, Chicago.

Cover and Program Design: Michaelis/Carpelis Design Associates, Inc.

Additional Design: Textart, Inc.

Production: Textart, Inc.
Michaelis/Carpelis Design Associates, Inc.

Illustration

Cover Illustration: Richard Bernal

Four-color airbrush: Brian Dugan, Mark Kaplan, Mary Ellen Senor

Poetry airbrush backgrounds: Mark Kaplan

Learning Center Logos: Rachel Geswaldo

Lesson Opener Panels: Lori Osiecki, 48, 78; Nicolai Punim, 60, 90; Marti Shohet, 54, 84; David Tillinghast, 42, 72; Andrea Winewski, 34, 66.

Four-color illustration: Pat Wong, 47, 71.

Black line art: Network Graphics, 35, 38, 43, 44, 49, 55, 61, 67, 73, 79, 81, 85, 94; Adam Weston, 58, 64, 65, 82, 88.

Photography

All photographs are by Macmillan/McGraw-Hill School Division (MMSD) except as noted below.

35: Ken Karp for MMSD. 41: Ken Karp for MMSD. 43: Scott Harvey for MMSD. 45: Ken Karp for MMSD. 46: Ken Karp for MMSD. 49: Scott Harvey for MMSD. 51: Scott Harvey for MMSD. 53: Scott Harvey for MMSD. 57: Ken Karp for MMSD. 63: Scott Harvey for MMSD. 65: Ken Karp for MMSD. 71: Ken Karp for MMSD. 73: Scott Harvey for MMSD. 75: Ken Karp for MMSD. 77: Ken Karp for MMSD. 79: Ken Karp for MMSD. 83: Ken Karp for MMSD. 86: Ken Karp for MMSD. 89: Scott Harvey for MMSD. 93: Ken Karp for MMSD. 98–104: Scott Harvey for MMSD. 105: Ken Karp for MMSD.

INDEX

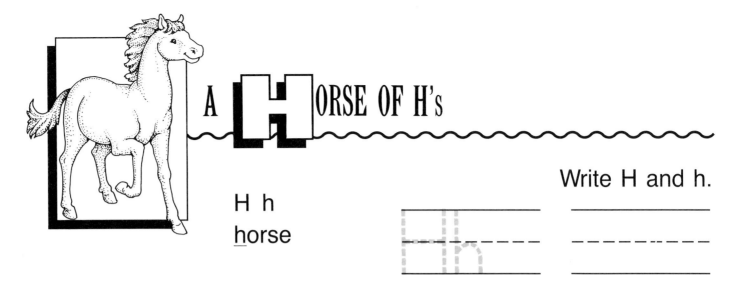

A **H**ORSE OF H's

H h
<u>h</u>orse

Write H and h.

<u>Pretend that you are taking a trip on a horse.</u>
What can you take with you?
You can only take things whose names begin like <u>horse</u>!
Cut out the pictures at the bottom. If the picture name
begins like <u>horse</u>, paste it on
the picture of the horse.

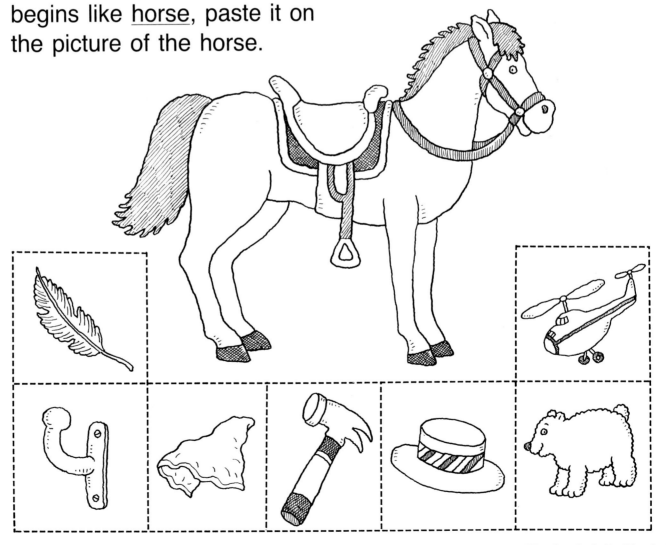

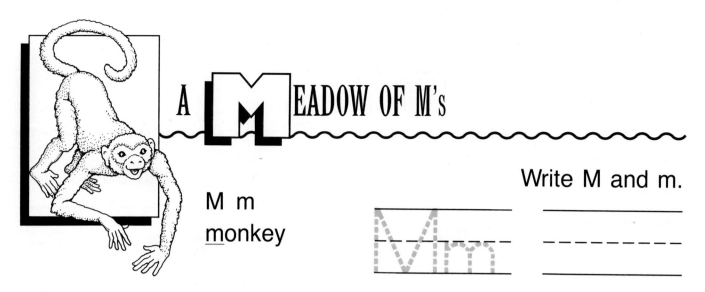

A **M** EADOW OF M's

M m
<u>m</u>onkey

Write M and m.

Mm

Monkey wants to start a meadow of M's.
Cut out the pictures at the bottom of the page.
Say each picture name. If the picture name
begins like <u>monkey</u>, paste it on the meadow.

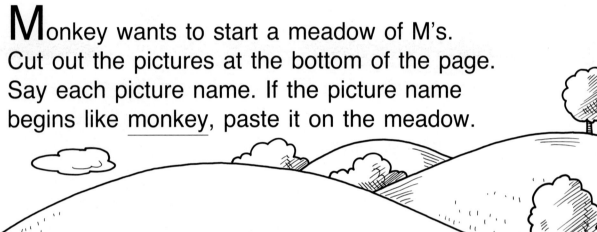